Pictorial
history

# of trains

history of trains

O.S.Nock

Sundial

Contents

Foreword

First published in 1976 by
Sundial Publications Limited
59 Grosvenor Street
London W1

Seventh impression, 1979

© 1976 Hennerwood Publications Limited

ISBN 0 904230 15 5

Produced by Mandarin Publishers Limited
Hong Kong

In writing and illustrating a pictorial history of trains, I would like to say a few words about its purpose and scope. This book traces the development of steam as I have seen it on my travels round the world during the past 50 years, and concentrates particularly on the magnificence of the working systems of steam railways and on the great engines still to be found in running order.

Modern diesels and electrics are included, but it was during the first 40 years of this century that the development and running of steam locomotives reached its height and it is this period that holds most fascination for train-lovers. Many trains designed at this time are still in regular use in European countries and have been photographed against some of the most magnificent scenery in the world. The railways of the United States, Australia, Japan, South Africa and India have provided me with equally interesting experiences and have yielded the spectacular photographic material included here. My sincere thanks are due to all the photographers who have contributed to this book.

O. S. Nock

Steam, diesel and electric in Britain

In this chapter on the country which saw the birth and early exploitation of the steam railway engine, we have as on a turntable come full circle. I examine, going clockwise from due North, the route to the North East; the South of England; the sphere of influence of the Great Western Railway; the westerly and central routes to the North West, over Shap and the Settle-Carlisle run respectively; and, finally, I look at the Scottish systems. So much for steam: but, as will be seen, the diesels and electrics, powerful as they are, have not been allowed to have it all their own way, for the public interest in preserving steam has grown constantly since steam, sadly, disappeared from the schedules of British Rail.

North East England Much of the first fourteen years of my life as a professional engineer was spent in offices overlooking King's Cross Station in London—not, it must be admitted, the most colourful part of the world of trains. But out of those grimy precincts went some of the most famous trains in history; and they drove north through a countryside that was an epitome of rural, farming England, past the great cathedrals of Peterborough, York and Durham, threading through the industrial North East, which was the very cradle of the steam locomotive, till they came out on the lonely and fascinating coastline of Northumberland. They climbed no dramatic mountain ranges in the process and crossed no greater river than the Tyne, by the King Edward Bridge at Newcastle. But whatever the country traversed by such trains as the *Queen of Scots*, the *Aberdonian*, and above all the *Flying Scotsman* may have lacked in spectacular scenery, their glamour was fully provided by the locomotives that hauled them throughout the age of steam.

From 1870 to the very end of steam traction some 95 years later there was never a more colourful range of locomotives than those hauling the Anglo-Scottish expresses out of King's Cross, and those that took them on from York in the days when the Great Northern and North Eastern were separate companies, though close allies in business.

It is fortunate beyond measure that so many examples of this great and picturesque mechanical engineering evolution have been preserved. Many of them can be seen in the National Railway Museum at York, while others are still in full working order and used for hauling special trains. The locomotives of the 1870s were as much *objets d'art* as pieces of hard-working machinery. Patrick Stirling of the Great Northern, who designed the elegant eight-foot single No. 1, refused to try a newer form of valve gear because it would spoil the look of his engine; and Edward Fletcher of the North

Left. The British High Speed Train (HST) came into service on the London—Swansea route in autumn 1976. Although advertised as being capable of 125 mph, it can in fact reach a considerably greater speed.

Top. The LNER 'A4' Pacific named after the designer *Sir Nigel Gresley* here carrying the former *Flying Scotsman* headboard in September 1975.

Above. The 'Merchant Navy' class *Union Castle*, No. 35002, seen here in BR livery near Honiton Tunnel, was one of 140 slab-sided 4-6-2s in three name classes introduced by the Southern Railway from the late 1930s onwards.

Eastern, who was an apprentice in Stephenson's works at Newcastle when the everfamous *Rocket* was built in 1829, designed the supremely decorated 2-4-0 No. 910 of 1872, which was in steam again at the 150th Anniversary parade in August 1975.

The chronology of Great Northern development is complete in preserved locomotives from 1898 onwards. The legendary large-boilered 'Atlantic' by H. A. Ivatt, No. 251, introduced in 1902, seems now to be finally retired to the quietude of the museum at York. She created something of a sensation, some 70 years ago, and still more so in traffic after she and her kind had been modernized by Sir Nigel Gresley; but that great engineer will always be best remembered for his 'Pacifics', and with three of them still in full working order, and the immortal, record-holding *Mallard* at York, their memory and their distinctive colours will remain for posterity. How *Mallard* attained 126 mph, and with it made the world record for steam traction that has not been surpassed, was an epic in itself. Before being retired she was much in demand for special trains and travelled far and wide in Great Britain, though her record in this respect was eclipsed by one of Gresley's earliest 'Pacifics', the *Flying Scotsman*, which made a long tour in Canada and the USA.

Flying Scotsman now carries the beautiful 'apple-green' livery that was standard for express passenger engines on the London and North Eastern Railway; but *Mallard* and the other two streamliners are in garter blue, adopted for this class, when the 'Coronation' high-speed express was put on between King's Cross and Edinburgh in 1937. It was a happy inspiration on the part of the LNER Board to name the hundredth 'Pacific' of Gresley after the designer; and the *Sir Nigel Gresley*, No. 4498, is still an active performer, and has been seen in many areas lately where the garter blue would have been unfamiliar in Sir Nigel's lifetime. The last of this family of locomotives is *Bittern*, one of that series, like *Mallard*, named after the fastest birds of the air. *Bittern* originally worked from Newcastle and was a familiar sight anywhere between London and Edinburgh.

Southern England Long before I worked near King's Cross I knew colourful trains from holidays before World War I on the Kentish coast; for on the boat trains that came sweeping down past the chalk cliffs of the Folkestone Warren and on to the old Admiralty Pier at Dover, were the Wainwright 4-4-0's of the South Eastern and Chatham Railway. Although I have travelled since far and wide on the railways of the world I do not think I have ever seen a more beautifully proportioned nor more tastefully decorated locomotive than the 'D'

The preserved Great Western giant No. 6000 *King George V* on a special train at Abergavenny in 1972. The engine carries the bell presented at the time of her visit to the U.S.A. in 1927 to attend the centenary celebrations of the Baltimore and Ohio Railroad.

class; and to the delight of all Southern enthusiasts one of these has been preserved and restored to all its original glory in the National Railway Museum.

Among many ardent railway enthusiasts William Stroudley was a patriarchal figure. It was he who introduced the famous 'Improved engine green', which was actually a beautiful mid-chrome yellow! It was not only on the Brighton and Portsmouth expresses that Stroudley's engines showed their colours. Local tank engines working through the South London suburbs, or over that unspeakable line through the Thames Tunnel, also sported the famous yellow; and woe betide the driver of those days who had a speck of dirt on his engine! They were all named mostly after stations on the line, though this could be unfortunate for the passenger who mistook the name of the engine for the destination of the train. Perhaps the most famous of all Brighton engines is *Gladstone* which deservedly has a place in the National Railway Museum.

The third constituent of the Southern was the London and South Western, which ran through the somnolent Wessex countryside. One of its chief mechanical engineers was that great, though irascible Scotsman, Dugald Drummond who was famous for his bad language to his staff and visitors alike. The beautiful locomotives that remain are mostly of his predecessor's design, that of William Adams, as much a character as Drummond although in a different way, who at one time had been engineer to the Sardinian Navy, before the days of the united Italy. One of Adams' London suburban tank engines works on the Bluebell Line in Sussex, while a magnificent specimen of his 4-4-0 express type is at York.

West of England When that remarkable engineer, I. K. Brunel, built the South Devon Railway beneath the red cliffs of Dawlish and Teignmouth, he certainly provided for all time a backdrop of vivid, majestic colouring that would ennoble the passage of any train, however utilitarian its individual engine and carriages might be on their own. But the Great Western engines of 70 years ago were far from utilitarian in their colouring, as can be seen from the splendid restoration of the *City of Truro* in 1957. This engine made a famous run in May 1904 with an Ocean Mail special from Plymouth, when she became the first engine in the world to reach 100 mph.

Her creator, George Jackson Churchward, one of the truly great engine designers of history, was no sentimentalist. Not only did he water down the one-time gay livery of Great Western locomotives, but he scrapped the last remaining express engine of Brunel's broad gauge that his predecessor had preserved – to make more space in Swindon works! Even with the simplified and less

The preserved Great Western 4-6-0 No. 4079 *Pendennis Castle*, passing in March 1974 through Gloucester with empty coaching stock en route to Hereford.

colourful livery, engines passing along the Dawlish–Teignmouth sea wall still looked ornate, with their copper-capped chimneys, polished brass safety-valve columns, and a handsome, if restrained, painting style in dark green. The style of Great Western locomotives remained individual and unchanged to the very end of the steam era, and astonishingly so in colour also – even though the nationalized British railways had one spell of painting the largest of them blue and the lesser lights in black. Today *Pendennis Castle*, *Burton Agnes Hall* and several more, up to the giant *King George V*, are in full working order, and can be seen hauling special trains. A little further west on the beautiful branch line from Paignton down to Kingswear the power today is entirely by preserved Great Western steam locomotives, maintained as before.

The home of the *King George V* is now at Hereford, and one of the favourite running grounds for this famous and far-travelled locomotive is over that beautiful route through the Welsh Border country, northwards through Leominster, Ludlow and Church Stretton to Shrewsbury. At that great junction contact is made with a line leading into the heart of Wales, where in the 1930s the Great Western faced something of a problem in locomotive power.

The very picturesque main line of the famous Cambrian Railways had then been incorporated in the GWR, and its track and bridges laid through much wild mountain country were light, and would not carry the larger standard engines. The 40-year-old 4-4-0s of the 'Duke' class needed replacement, and an ingenious compromise was made by taking the frames of some almost-as-old but serviceable engines which were too heavy as they stood, and putting on 'Duke'-type boilers. These hybrids, using frames from the 'Bulldog' class, became nicknamed the 'Duke-dogs'. They did yeoman work in Central Wales, and one is now preserved on the Bluebell Line.

The Western Region has recently been in the forefront of new developments with the introduction in 1976 of the High Speed Train. This is a multiple unit train of sophisticated design, powered by diesel-electric engines in the end units, and intended for a speed of 125 mph. The first service operated by these trains was between London and Bristol, a route facing competition from the private car. Some criticism was expressed on the wisdom of investing many millions of pounds in order to cut the journey by 15 minutes, but early indications were that, whatever the economic arguments, the HST was a step forward in fostering a favourable public opinion towards passenger train travel.

The HST was expected to be followed by a true high speed train, the Advanced Passenger Train. This, already running in prototype form, has such novelties as a suspension which keeps the wheel flanges away

from the rails even on curves to reduce friction, and a tilting body to absorb centrifugal forces on curves. Passive tilting bodies were not new, but, starting in Germany in 1968, an active tilt was developed, in which power was applied to the pivoting bodies so that the tilt could be initiated before the centrifugal pressures were felt, thereby subjecting passengers to much gentler forces. The APT has this active tilt, and thus can run at high speeds over routes whose curves have not been eased in anticipation.

North West England When the West Coast group of early railways, the London and Birmingham, the Liverpool and Manchester, and the Grand Junction, sought to extend their activities to the Scottish border the

great pioneer George Stephenson was quite deterred by the prospect of having to carry a railway through the Lake District or over the Westmorland fells to get from Lancaster to Carlisle. Instead, he proposed crossing Morecambe Bay and making a long detour round the Cumberland coast. His one-time pupil, Joseph Locke, was called in to advise and he recommended the great trunk route over the Shap Fells that was actually built.

However, the route was made much more difficult than it might have been as Locke had a great aversion to tunnels. Perhaps it was the ghastly experience he had had in taking over the uncompleted Woodhead tunnel on the line from Manchester to Sheffield, in the building of which many

lives were lost. But on the Lancaster and Carlisle line he could have obtained much easier gradients by going from Kendal up Long Sleddale, tunnelling under the ridge, and coming out beside Haweswater. Instead he took the line in a detour eastwards over an intermediate summit at Grayrigg and into the gorge of the river Lune. But while it was tough going for the locomotives, the mountain scenery was sublime. Before it was finished, the great 'West Coast' group to the south had amalgamated to become the London and North Western Railway, the 'Premier Line' of all Britain, and that company operated the Lancaster and Carlisle from the outset and eventually absorbed it.

The engines of the North Western had a fascination that was not surpassed in the days of the old companies. Fortunately there is a very famous example of a nineteenth-century North Western engine preserved in the 2-4-0 loco *Hardwicke*, (see p 14). Until the early 1900s all trains of any weight required two engines to get them over the 915 ft altitude of Shap Summit, and there the speed would rarely be more than 30 mph with ordinary express trains. But when *Hardwicke* was taking the Highland tourist train on the last night of the great Race to the North it was 'all or nothing'. The load had been cut to no more than three coaches, and she ran the entire 141 miles from Crewe to Carlisle in 126 minutes, an average speed of 67 mph – Shap included!

Above. A Great Western Society Special from Didcot to Tyseley (Birmingham), leaving Heyford, hauled by the restored 4-6-0 No. 6998 *Burton Agnes Hall.*

Below. London-Plymouth express on the Teignmouth sea wall, with the picturesque Parson and Clark Rocks in the distance. The locomotive is a Class 52 diesel-hydraulic No. 1065 *Western Consort*.
Bottom. The northbound 'Devonian' shortly after the start of its long run from South Devon to Leeds, passing along the sea wall between Teignmouth and Dawlish, hauled by one of the 'Peak' class diesel-electric locomotives.

Right. On the one-time broad gauge main line of Brunel: one of the Western Region diesel hydraulic locomotives of the Warship class, *Daring*, passing through Sydney Gardens, Bath, with a London to Bristol express.

What that little engine did on the night of 21–22 August 1895 remains one of the greatest epics of railway history.

The great 'gable' of Shap, 31½ miles up from Morecambe Bay and 31½ miles down to Carlisle, governed locomotive practice on the West Coast route to the very end of steam days. For the London and North Western Railway Crewe works built larger and larger engines, until in 1913 one of C. J. Bowen Cooke's 'Claughton' 4-6-0s made a record that ranks almost with *Hardwicke's* epic of eighteen years earlier. Tearing through the Lune Gorge and making an all-out charge on Shap there was registered in the dynamometer testing car the highest horsepower of any British locomotive up to the time of grouping in 1923. And what a setting for an outstanding mechanical achievement, in the magnificent scenery of this Lune Gorge, with the railway carried high above the torrent and the fells towering on both sides of the line. Sadly no one thought to take a photograph of the occasion. Only the scientific records remain.

In the 1920s the London and North Western became part of the London Midland and Scottish; 'Claughtons' gave place to 'Royal Scots' and the colour of the express engines became red. But still the majestic scene remained, where the only noise was that of an express running through the gorge or an occasional car making its way up the narrow road over the fells. Today all is changed. The M6 motorway was driven through the valley, at a higher level than the railway, and although much was done after the construction was completed to heal the scars of cutting and embankment, the roar of the highway is hardly ever absent. Things have also changed on the railways. There was a transition stage in the first years of nationaliztion, when the 'Britannia' class 'Pacifics' came to supplement the former LMS types, and then came the diesels. Speed did not noticeably increase until the early 1970s when as a foretaste of electrification some greatly accelerated trains were put on which needed *two* diesels to keep time.

The metamorphosis since 1974 has been complete. In former days we would sit by the line looking westward towards the ruins of Shap Abbey, and unhurriedly point

our cameras towards a 'Royal Scot', or a Stanier 'Duchess' struggling up the last four miles at 1 in 75 to Shap Summit. Today the overhead electric wires, carrying 25,000 volts, are remarkably unobtrusive in that vast landscape; but what tremendous power they contain! The 'Royal Scot' express of today is of twelve coaches as before, but instead of puffing up that incline at a bare 30 mph its speed is at least 85 mph, and on one recorded occasion was 95 mph.

The Settle and Carlisle railway Until 1876 the beautiful route over Shap was the only railway from the South and Midlands of England to Carlisle, and the Midland Railway had to send such Scottish traffic as it could over a most unlikely way. It had control of a subsidiary line known as the 'Little North Western' that ran from Skipton, in the West Riding, towards Lancaster, and at a wild moorland namesake of London's great Clapham Junction it pioneered a line up the Lune Valley, with the intention of making a junction with the 'big' North Western at Low Gill, and so feeding into the Shap route to Carlisle. But in the 'cut and thrust' of railway politics in mid-Victorian times the 'big' North Western got in first and built a branch line of its own southwards from Low Gill. The result was an end-on junction with the Midland branch at Ingleton. Furthermore it made interchange of traffic so awkward that the Midland determined to have its own line to

Above. The veteran London and North Western 2-4-0 of the 1895 Race to Aberdeen, No. 790 *Hardwicke*, in steam at Carnforth after her restoration to running condition in July 1975.

Below. Early morning on the Shap Incline: an overnight express from London to Glasgow climbing the 1 in 75 gradient, hauled by a Stanier 'Black Five' 4-6-0 with a second engine banking in the rear.

Right. On Robert Stephenson's Chester and Holyhead Railway: a Stanier 'Black Five' 4-6-0 passing through the arch in the mediaeval town wall of Conway, with a Holyhead to Manchester Express.

the Scottish border. Thus was conceived the magnificent Settle and Carlisle railway.

It was no easy task to find a way through the dales of north-west Yorkshire and Westmorland. The new route had to be competitive in speed. There was no case for a cheap mountain route: it was to be a fast express route, by which the Midland could match the best London and North Western times to Carlisle, and north-west of Skipton was an area of deep valleys, rugged mountain ridges and sedgy moorland, all subject to the worst extremes of weather. From the south there was a possible route up North Ribblesdale, but this ended, after fourteen miles, in the waste of Blea Moor. From Carlisle there was the Eden Valley, extending in all its north-country variations for nearly 50 miles to the 1,167-ft high Aisgill Moor. But between Blea Moor and Aisgill lay the high Pennines, and C. S. Sharland, the surveyor, had to find an alignment that could be built into a fast express route. The outcome was one of the most dramatic pieces of main-line railway in Britain: tunnels through limestone rock; viaducts so exposed to the winds that stonemasons sometimes had to cease work for fear of being blown off the scaffolding; bog where there seemed to be no solid bottom on which to build an embankment. But all the difficulties were overcome eventually, and in 1876 the line was opened to traffic—a notable advance.

The original specification was fulfilled to

Above left. The last steam special operated by British Railways over the Settle and Carlisle Line, on August 11, 1968, is here seen approaching Aisgill summit, Westmorland, hauled by two Stanier 'Black Five' 4-6-0s.
Below left. The Channel Islands boat train, Weymouth to Wolverhampton, climbing the very steep gradient past Upwey Wishing Well Halt, hauled by one of the 'Hymek' diesel hydraulic locomotives.

Above. On the Settle and Carlisle line: a diesel-hauled Leeds to Glasgow express ascending the 'Long Drag' from Settle to Blea Moor in winter, with the flat-topped Ingleborough Hill in the background.
Below. One of the celebrated Stanier 'Black Five' 4-6-0s on a Glasgow-Dundee express near Gleneagles, Perthshire.

Below. The restored Midland Compound 4-4-0 No. 1000, in the form which she took when she was rebuilt in 1914 from the original Johnson compound of 1902.

Right. One of the Stanier 'Jubilee' class three cylinder 4-6-0s of the LMS, No. 5690 *Leander*, restored to its original livery and photographed in York Station in 1975, on the way to Darlington for the 150th anniversary pageant.

the letter. There was not a single speed restriction between Settle and Carlisle, and the Midland express trains of 70 years ago went uphill at 40 mph, crossed the central tableland at 60–65 mph and went downhill on one occasion at a maximum of 96 mph in the early days of the Midland compound 4-4-0 engines. The first of these, now numbered 1000, is one of the treasured exhibits in the National Railway Museum at York. The design was specially prepared to provide ample power for the long uphill stretches of the Settle and Carlisle line; and in those days when each engine had its own crew, and no other, the first engine, then numbered 2631, was stationed at Carlisle and the second one at Leeds. They were exclusive to this route. The line has always been a challenge, and when the LMS was formed in 1923 competitive testing of engines from the former individual companies took place between Carlisle and Leeds. In the mountain country of North Ribblesdale; in climbing to Aisgill; or in racing across that high-level stretch overlooking Garsdale, Dentdale and across the great viaducts and beside the snow fences, many locomotive reputations were made and broken.

After the formation of British Railways in 1948 the Settle and Carlisle became more than ever a proving ground. Testing was much more scientific; the engines to be tried were drawn from wider fields, and the climax came when one of the great Stanier 'Pacifics', the *Duchess of Gloucester*, was driven practically to the limit of her boiler. Then, just as the Shap route had, in 1913, witnessed the highest output of power registered in the old days before grouping, so on the 'Long Drag' from Settle Junction up to Blea Moor the *Duchess* sustained the highest rate of continuous evaporation ever recorded in a British locomotive. Whereas normal passenger trains are now of about 400 to 450 tons, on this test a train of 900 tons was taken up to Blea Moor at 30 mph.

Nowadays, the loads on this route are about 300 tons, and the diesels make short work of the long 1 in 100 gradients. The climbing speed is not much less than 60 mph. But although there is little sound, and no smoke and steam to mark their comings and goings, this remote high-altitude world of trains still has its own magic. I do not think I have ever equalled the thrill of a ride which I had on the second engine of a double header, when the leader was an old Midland 4-4-0, and in the teeth of a mountain storm we tore across the high ground from Blea Moor at nearly 70 mph.

Bearing in mind the countless miles of service that lies behind them it is fascinating to walk round the National Railway Museum and see such a variety of famous steam locomotives grouped around the central turntable. This is no workaday roundhouse improvised for the job, but a complete rebuilding of the old steam running sheds to provide the spaciousness essential to view these magnificent relics to the best advantage. There are more Midland engines at Leicester and some famous Great Westerns, including the *City of Truro*, at Swindon; but York is now the focal point of England's railway history, as is appropriate.

Scotland It is now time to travel into Scotland, where it is hard to decide whether excellence of mechanical design or the artistic elegance of the trains themselves is the more impressive. Beautiful locomotives of the Caledonian, Great North of Scotland, Highland, and North British railways were restored to their original condition and maintained to run numerous special excursions. Sometimes when the loads were heavy two of them would run in partnership; and when these excursions led over the West Highland line, over the Callander and Oban and down the wild Sou'West 'road' from Girvan to Stranraer, the mountains, moors and lochs, in all the glorious vicissitudes of West Coast weather, provided a magnificent background to the vivid sky-blue of the Caledonian 4-2-2 No. 123, the rich green of the *Gordon Highlander*, the distinctive greenish brown of *Glen Douglas*, and above all the Jones 4-6-0, in Stroudley's Brighton-style 'yellow'.

These were all famous engines, fully deserving preservation. The Caledonian '123' ran daily in the Race to the North, taking the Euston flyer from Carlisle to Edinburgh for 23 days in succession – never in more than 110 minutes for 100½ very hilly miles, and once in a brilliant 102½ minutes, in 1888! The 'Jones Goods' was the first British locomotive of the 4-6-0 type, specially introduced for the long climbs

Right. The Caledonian 4-2-2 single No. 123, a famous runner in the London-Edinburgh 'race' of 1888, is here seen near Cleland working a special train of two restored Caledonian carriages on the former Caledonian route from Glasgow to Edinburgh.

over the Grampian Mountains on the main line from Perth to Inverness, while the massive 'Glen' class of the North British were built for the most scenic route in all Britain, the West Highland, which wove an exceedingly mountainous way from the Firth of Clyde, at Helensburgh, up to Fort William and then out through the Rough Bounds and beside the Road to the Isles to Mallaig. *Glen Douglas* ran that road for many years, and when the loads were heavy a pair of 'Glens' was in my experience an unbeatable combination.

Scottish railroading is not all hard slogging on steep, winding gradients. The Caledonian main line from Carlisle, over Beattock summit and into Clydesdale, was a speedway as early as 1888, and now electrification has transformed it as thoroughly as it has done for Shap. A memorable sight, soon after a summer dawn, was of a heavy overnight sleeping-car express from London toiling up the Beattock Bank – a big 'Duchess' class 'Pacific' at its head, and a sturdy little tank engine pushing in rear,

the bark of their exhausts echoing and their steam hanging in long trails in the morning air. They would be making good time if they climbed that 10 miles of 1 in 75 gradient in less than 20 minutes.

There were many times when the men on the engine would not have appreciated the early morning colour and mountain beauty of the Beattock Bank. Even on the finest days, soon after dawn a mist would come rolling down from the hills. The damp on the rails would make them slippery, and then nothing that the most skilful driver could do would avoid wheel slip. It would be no use trying to make use of the 2,000 horsepower or more latent in the steam generated in the boiler; there was nothing for it but to take things quietly and let the engine herself find the speed at which she could keep her feet. That is why on so many occasions even the most capable of drivers with the finest of engines were prudent enough to stop at Beattock station at the foot of the incline and take the help of a pusher engine in the rear. There have been

Below. The first example of the 4-6-0 type in Great Britain, the 'Jones Goods' of the Highland Railway, working a special train of two restored Caledonian coaches. It is seen here on one of the most difficult parts of its own line, the long climb from Blair Atholl to its summit in the Grampian Mountains at the Pass of Druimauchdar, 1484 ft above sea level, and the highest railway summit in Britain.
Above right. A one-time rival route from Glasgow to Edinburgh—now the *only* main inter-city line between them—with the restored North British 4-4-0 No. 256 *Glen Douglas* working a special train near Ratho. The 'Glen' class 4-4-0s were designed especially for the West Highland line, and worked there for more than 30 years.
Below right. The restored Great North of Scotland Railway 4-4-0 No. 49 *Gordon Highlander* with a Glasgow to Edinburgh special, on the former Caledonian route, again near Cleland.

some heroic attacks on this great summit. The climb from the north side is not so severe, and one Sunday in 1939 when a maximum power test was in progress the 'Pacific' engine *Duchess of Abercorn*, hauling a huge load of 610 tons, approached Beattock summit in a blinding snowstorm, yet charged over the top at 63 mph, recording a mighty 3,333 horsepower in the process.

Coming up from the south, where steam and diesel trains were allowed 20 minutes to climb that severe 10 miles, the 25,000-volt electrics are now given only *seven minutes*, which means that instead of grinding uphill at 30 mph they now have to average 85 mph. In earlier days motorists on the adjacent highway could leave the trains standing: in fact an enthusiastic photographer could 'shoot' the *Royal Scot* somewhere down near Auchencastle, jump into his car, and have plenty of time to photograph it again as it pounded laboriously up the last miles to the summit. Not so nowadays as the electrics flash past on their way up the glen. But even with all the modern sophistication they can still be hindered by the weather on

Below. A general-utility 'Black Five' 4-6-0 of the LMS on an eastbound goods train between Alloa and Bogside in Scotland.

Below left. Southbound across the Tay Bridge: a double-headed diesel-hauled express from Aberdeen to Edinburgh approaches the Fife shore, with a fine panorama of Dundee in the background.

Above. The two restored Caledonian Railway coaches forming a special train leaving Princes Street station Edinburgh hauled by a British Railways standard Class '2' 2-6-0 No. 78046.
Below. Winter in the West Highlands: a diesel hauled train from Fort William to Glasgow is pictured crossing one of the viaducts between Tyndrum Upper and Crianlarich, Perthshire.
Above right. A veteran North British 0-6-0 goods engine No. 65345 approaching Bathgate with a local coal train.

the Beattock Bank. I was riding in the cab of the *Royal Scot* electric locomotive one day, and we were storming up the gradient at 88 mph. Then there was a shower of rain. The wheels slipped at once, and in seconds we were down to 75 mph. This was still, in fact, a very impressive and exciting speed to climb such a gradient, but it was a dramatic instance of what the weather can still do.

Preserved steam Today, although no regularly scheduled steam operation on British Railways exists, a venture launched more than a quarter of a century ago by a band of enthusiasts with skill, railway know-how, and sound financial backing has proved the catalyst for a whole series of projects for preservation, providing in working order not only individual locomotives but whole sections of railway. How the little narrow-gauge Tal-y-llyn Railway in central Wales, only 6¾ miles long, was saved from extinction was an epic in itself. It was of course an entirely self-contained unit; but its success led to others, like the resuscitation of the derelict Festiniog Railway, which was

literally rusting away. Its track was overgrown with weeds and saplings, its locomotives and rolling stock were rotting away amid derelict sheds and workshops and becoming more and more exposed to the weather as roofs and walls collapsed. It was originally built to transport slates, and speed was of no consequence. Now its present locomotives are beautifully maintained and very popular with all enthusiasts. But then there came the great modernization plan for British Railways, which included the wholesale closing down of many unremunerative branch lines, and the eventual complete supersession of steam traction; and with the examples of the Tal-y-llyn and the Festiniog before them a whole crop of preservation schemes was mooted, not of narrow gauge, but of standard gauge lines, to be operated by time-experienced locomotives and rolling stock. Not all the schemes propounded have yet come to fruition, but then as the time came for famous locomotives to be withdrawn and sold for scrap a collateral movement for preservation developed. From

these two sources, quite apart from the establishment of the National Railway Museum at York, a number of beautiful and highly colourful enterprises have been firmly established.

That many of the private enterprise preservation schemes for working sections of railway lie in districts away from the areas of intense traffic, which would in other circumstances have compelled the closing down of the lines altogether, has been most fortunate from the scenic point of view. One could not, for example, find a more picturesque West Country branch line than that of the former Great Western Railway from Paignton to Kingswear, climbing first onto the cliffs overlooking Torbay, and then after breasting the ridge making a sinuous course down the hillside above the river Dart to the water's edge at Kingswear. The Severn Valley line between Kidderminster and Bridgnorth runs through continuously lovely scenery, while the North Yorkshire Moors Railway is keeping alive one of the most picturesque parts of

the former North Eastern Railway route from Pickering to Whitby. In all these areas locomotives saved from the scrap-heap have been restored by enthusiasts with full technical experience and ability and are going about their new duties lovingly polished and maintained, providing scenes definitely more colourful than in the days when they were struggling forlornly on lines officially discredited up to the time of closure.

Then there are the 'steam centres', based on certain running sheds that were no longer required under the general moderniz-ation of the British Railways motive-power fleet. These have been taken over by various societies and provide areas where preserved locomotives may be steamed without en-croaching upon the ordinary running lines. They also provide bases for the housing and maintenance of those locomotives which on particular occasions are allowed to work special trains along routes over which steam haulage is still permitted. There is the large Didcot depot of the Great Western Society, where a considerable variety of historic coaching stock is also maintained and, in some cases, restored from a condition of serious decay. When these depots stage an open day the colourful world of trains is manifested in the most delightful way. Then again at Tyseley, near Birmingham, formerly an important Great Western steam shed, it is not merely a case of preservation. Machinery has been installed for the under-taking of quite heavy repair work, and with considerable space in the yard an open-day at Tyseley, with locomotives of other railways beside those of the Great Western in steam, is something to remember.

One of the most famous of all British steam locomotives, the *King George V* of the Great Western, was scheduled for presentation as a museum piece and for a long time was stored in a remote corner of the old stock shed at Swindon. But a group of enthusiasts in the West Midlands, with

Above left. The Bluebell Line: a beautiful example of the later Brighton engine livery on the 'R4' class 0-6-2 tank engine *Birch Grove*, near Waterworks.
Above middle. The North Yorkshire Moors Railway: the Kitson 0-6-2 tank engine, formerly belonging to the Lambton Railway, climbing from Grosmont to Goathland.
Below left. The preserved LNER 'V2' class 2-6-2 No. 4771 *Green Arrow* on a special eastbound from Carnforth to Leeds, passing Wennington.
Above right. On the Severn Valley Railway, at Eardington, the former War Department Austerity 2-10-0, now named *Gordon*, on a southbound goods train.
Below right. A striking double-header on the Keighley and Worth Valley line: the restored Lancashire and Yorkshire 0-6-0 No. 951 of 1887, pilots the LMS 2-6-2T No. 41241 on Mytholmes Viaduct in March 1975.

the enthusiastic backing of H P Bulmer Ltd, the cider manufacturers, formed the '6000 Association', and the engine was restored to full working order; it is now based on a special siding and shed in Bulmer's works. The great engine is now seen on occasions working special trains on the permitted routes, though because of its Great Western ancestry these are less extensive than those permitted to some other notable locomotives. The former GWR inherited from broad gauge days of Brunel a somewhat more liberal loading gauge than those of most other railways, and the 'King' class locomotives were built to take advantage of this. At present, the *King George V* is not permitted to run over any of the former LMS or

Southern lines because of this.

One of the most remarkable steam concentration points in Great Britain is the junction of Carnforth, on the west coast main line about six miles north of Lancaster in the north-east corner of Morecambe Bay. In pre-grouping days Carnforth was a triple junction, where the cross-country line of the Midland from Skipton and the cities of the West Riding crossed the London and North Western main line about half a mile north of the station and then came round on an exceedingly sharp curve to join the Furness Railway and come into the station from the west. 'Steamtown' is now on the site of the old Furness running sheds. At first it was intended to be a kind of north country

Tyseley with plans to include one or two unusual locomotives, but with the establishment of the cross-country line from Leeds, Steamtown has become an active base of operations for a great variety of trips. The ever-famous Gresley 'Pacific' *Flying Scotsman* has found its home there, together with the companion mixed-traffic 2-6-2 *Green Arrow*, while in addition to certain LMS engines there is the notable addition of a French 'Pacific' of the Paris, Lyons and Mediterranean type.

Steamtown, at Carnforth, played a very important part in the celebrations of the 150th anniversary of the opening of the Stockton and Darlington Railway in 1975 and those of the centenary of passenger

traffic on the far-famed Settle and Carlisle line of the Midland Railway in 1976.

When the historic LNWR 2-4-0 *Hardwicke* was put into working order once again so that she could take part in the anniversary pageant in September 1975 running under her own steam, she was taken for a trial run down the Furness line as far north as Sellafield. She revisited Carnforth at the time of the Settle and Carlisle centenary celebrations in May 1976, and seeing her there the thoughts of many may well have turned in imagination to the night of 22 August 1895 when at a time recorded as 11.39¾ pm she hurtled through on the Aberdeen racing train in the course of her record 67.2 mph run from Crewe to Carlisle.

The famous preserved Midland compound No. 1000 was also a familiar object at Carnforth in 1976. In company with *Hardwicke* she came across from the National Railway Museum to participate in the Settle and Carlisle festivities and, in partnership with one of the celebrated Stanier 'Black Five' 4-6-0s, was to have headed some of the special trains run on that occasion. Unfortunately they both failed in the shed and their places were taken by the *Hardwicke* and the *Flying Scotsman*. The Midland ran an excursion over the Furness Line from Carnforth to Sellafield and back. This is one of the many enterprising projects of the '6000 Association'.

Left. On the Wemyss Private Railway, Fife: an 0-6-0 tank engine No. 20 moving coal in Methil Yards.
Above. On the Keighley and Worth Valley Railway, in the Brontë Country, the last of all steam locomotives built for British Railways, the '9F' 2-10-0 No. 92220 *Evening Star* is seen here near Oakworth, on the climb from Keighley to Oxenhope in April 1974. This engine is now in the National Railway Museum at York.
Below. Forlorn last days of steam: two 2-6-4 tank engines, and a 'Britannia' class Pacific No. 70027 with nameplate removed at Manningham shed, Bradford.

Europe
West Germany

In the days when the many independent states were brought together by Bismarck in the newly constituted German Empire at the end of the Franco-Prussian war of 1870–1, there was a host of small and largely unconnected railways all over the land. Nowhere did these railways intersect, duplicate one another, and otherwise sprawl out more than in the Rhineland. After 1871 Bismarck tried to nationalize them all; but resistance in the southern states was too strong, even for him, and the railways of Baden and Bavaria in particular remained independent. Most of those in the north were brought under the control of Prussia, but with strong local administrations running them. The only group that was fully nationalized was the unfortunate Alsace–Lorraine system, in the territory annexed from France after the war, which had the prefix 'Imperial' added to its Germanized title. So far as technical developments were concerned it was Prussia and Bavaria that henceforth made the running – each in a way that had influences far beyond the frontiers of Germany.

Of all the railway networks in pre-Imperial days the one in the Rhineland, southwards from Cologne to Frankfurt, is by far the most fascinating. There are, of course, great centres of industrial railway

activity amid the cities of the Ruhr, where notable technological achievements in freight handling and traffic control have been made; but for one of the most interesting and picturesque railway rides he could wish for down the Rhine, the railway enthusiast should make the journey southwards from Cologne.

The principal express trains usually take the left bank of the Rhine, leaving the right bank for the freights. There are, nevertheless, numerous junctions and river crossings, and between high hills, stepped with vineyards, one can switch from one side to the other. There is hardly a valley with its river feeding into the Rhine that does not have its own railway, and some of these are far from being country branch lines. One of the most leisurely ways of seeing railway activity in its entirety is to travel by one of the beautiful river steamers; then the trains on both banks can be readily seen, and although one is rarely near enough to see the actual numbers, an enthusiastic 'spotter' could have a busy enough time noting the types of locomotive and the loads they were hauling, whether goods or passenger.

German steam locomotives, whether emanating from Prussia or Bavaria, were functional and efficient. Prussia's greatest contribution to the worldwide development

of the steam locomotive came from a scientist who was not originally a railwayman at all, Dr Wilhelm Schmidt of Berlin, who in the 1890s was developing the use of superheated steam. If steam was used just as it was generated, in the way hitherto accepted on every locomotive that had been built since the days of Richard Trevithick, 90 years earlier, it was *wet* no matter at what pressure it was generated; and there were also problems of condensation. If, after the steam was generated, it was heated further (superheated), the risk of condensation was lessened; it became much more fluid and its volume was increased. It was on locomotives of the Prussian State railways that Schmidt first applied his superheaters. His early experiments brought no more than moderate success, but from 1912 onwards there was hardly a main-line locomotive built anywhere in the world without a superheater.

The development in Bavaria was less obvious at first, but of great importance. In the chapter dealing with the railways of France mention will be made of Alfred de Glehn and his work on the compound locomotive. Now, down in Munich, at the famous firm of Maffei, another form of four-cylinder compound was being produced. De Glehn deliberately divided the drive between two axles in order to lessen the stresses in the axles themselves and in the bearings. Maffei arranged his compounds so that all four cylinders drove on to the same axle. There would seem at first to be a contradiction and a recession in practice in this, even though the driving axles themselves were made very strong and generous bearing surfaces were provided. But there was another vital factor involved.

Locomotives were getting large and heavy by the early years of the twentieth century and were reaching the limit which the civil engineer could accept on the track and bridges. These limits had evolved largely as a result of practical experience, not from any very scientific calculations; but at that time the more academically minded of engineers were investigating the effects of unbalanced forces in the moving parts of locomotives, and Maffei's layout with all four cylinders driving on to the same axle gave an almost perfectly balanced machine. Civil engineers on the continent of Europe were prepared to accept heavier

A West German 2-10-0, no. 051 0578, climbing from Neuenmarkt Wirsberg to Marktschorgast on the 07.06 Neuenmarkt-Wirsberg to Hof—one of many locos fitted with tender cabs.

axle loads with engines designed in this way, and this attitude proved of inestimable value to the Netherlands State Railways when they wanted to introduce larger and heavier locomotives in 1910.

After World War I, and the nationalization of all the German railways under the Republic, much attention was devoted to highly spectacular diesel railcar services, such as the *Flying Hamburger*; but steam remained the solid backbone of the entire operation, and it became even more so during World War II. The emphasis, as everywhere else among the European belligerents, was on freight, and a remarkable feat of locomotive designing and construction was carried out by German engineers. Before the war a very powerful freight engine of the 2-10-0 type had been successfully introduced. This was essentially a heavy main-line engine, and because of its weight there were many important lines over which it could not work. So a lighter version of the same design was produced and construction of both proceeded simultaneously. As the war situation developed, however, and many more locomotives were needed in countries controlled or overrun

by the military campaigns, a decision was taken to produce a general service 'war locomotive', a *Kriegslok*, that would have the widest possible route availability.

Because of the need to conserve supplies of all metals, and particularly the choicer grades needed for aircraft and other direct munitions of war, the design of the lightweight 2-10-0 was examined in the closest detail to see where metal could be saved. The original 'Series 50' was a very powerful engine for its overall weight, with tender, of 144 tons; but by dispensing with everything not absolutely essential in a *Kriegslok* no less than 27 tons of metal was saved in making the 'Series 52', and eventually more than 10,000 of these locomotives were built – many in Austria and Czechoslovakia. It is not surprising that they are still very familiar objects on the railways of West Germany and elsewhere in Central Europe. All working steam locomotives in West Germany today are black with red wheels; but the attractive green livery of the Bavarian State railways has been restored on one of the Maffei 'Pacific' engines now preserved in Munich, the Bavarian capital and railway headquarters.

Below. The *Rheingold* express, hauled by a Class 103 electric locomotive, passes through the suburbs of Düsseldorf. So named because much of its route is through the Rhine valley, it is an international express linking the Hook of Holland and Geneva.

Europe

France

From whatever angle one likes to regard them, and at whatever period in their long history, the railways of France provide a vivid and fascinating study. Generally the liveries of locomotives and carriages in the independent days up to 1938 were rather dull, though among locomotives there were a few startling exceptions such as the Forquenot 2-4-2s of the Paris–Orleans Railway, with their polished brass jacketed boilers, while the wind-cutter 4-4-os of the Paris, Lyons and Mediterranean were distinctive enough from their strange external appearance. There was nothing in France to rival the blues, reds and yellows of contemporary British locomotives, not to mention the gay colour schemes to be seen all over Holland.

What French steam lacked aesthetically however, it more than made up for in the soundness, albeit complexity, of its engineering and in the personalities of its men. They copied, with long-sustained enthusiasm, the precepts of the celebrated 'stern-wheelers' of the English designer Thomas Russell Crampton, which had a single pair of large-diameter driving wheels at the extreme rear end, with the driver and fireman ensconced between the wheels. The Northern Railway took another English design, by Archibald Sturrock of the Great Northern Railway, a 2-4-0 of 1866; it was a massively built thing, and after the French had developed it into a 4-4-0 they found it

Right. French National Railways: one of the most famous steam locomotive classes of all time, the Chapelon rebuilt Pacifics, SNCF–G 231-E class, originating on the Paris–Orleans Railway, here seen in the last years of French steam on a Nord express.
Opposite. One of the former PLM Pacifics–Class '23-K' no. 2, on a 'rapide' from Calais to Paris near Hesdigneul.

would stand thrashing *à l'outrance* and the class became known as the 'Outrance' – in other words, the 'all-out engines'. But there is a limit to what even the best-designed machinery will stand, and thrashing *à l'outrance* sometimes led to broken crank axles. This brought about one of the most important technical developments in steam locomotive history.

It was a time when engineers all over the world were seeking ways in which the thermal efficiency might be increased and coal consumption thereby reduced. Two-stage, or compound, expansion was being introduced on many railways, and on the Northern of France, in a fruitful collaboration between Alfred de Glehn and an

English engineer, then practising in Belfort, the compound principle was applied to a locomotive generally of the Outrance type, but with four cylinders instead of two. Instead of thrusting all the power for traction through one axle the drive was divided. The high-pressure cylinders were outside and drove the rear pair of wheels, while the low-pressure cylinders drove the leading pair. Thus the heavy stresses occurring in the Outrance type were avoided and the risk of broken crank axles lessened to a degree that was minimal. From the pioneer engine of the de Glehn four-cylinder compound type, which is fortunately preserved in the French Railway Museum at Mulhouse, Alsace, an entire dynasty of

locomotives followed, leading up to the outstanding Chapelon 'Pacifics' of the Paris–Orleans Railway, dating from 1929, and considered by many connoisseurs of steam locomotive practice to be the finest ever in the entire history of this machine.

Not all the star performers of the steam era in France came from the Northern and the Orleans railways. The Paris, Lyons and Mediterranean Railway had a long and illustrious tradition of locomotive working, and as its main line not only extended from Paris to Marseilles but continued thence along the Côte d'Azur to the Italian frontier at Ventimiglia, the locomotives of the PLM made their running in country of scenic splendour. To reach Marseilles they had to

cross the Rhône delta and in level and very exposed country survive the tremendous force of the Mistral wind. Thick hedges of cypress trees were grown alongside the line, and the powerful four-cylinder compound 4-4-0 and 4-6-0s express locomotives, known as the 'wind-cutters', had semi-streamlined fairings at the front and behind the boiler mountings to lessen the effect of the wind.

Beside the sombre browns, greys, dark greens and blacks of French steam locomotives the modern electric and diesel locomotives are highly colourful. And as with steam practice of old, the modern motive power of the French National railways is second to none in its technical quality. It is since the end of World War II that such remarkable development has taken place. Until then the lines converted to electric traction, notably the Paris–Tours section of the Orleans Railway, presented a rather dull spectacle of uninspiring 'juice boxes', as they were often called, excellent though their technical performance was from the outset. Then came the postwar decision to adopt 25,000 volts alternating current, instead of the 1,500 volts direct current used on the Orleans, on the first stages of PLM electrification, and in Great Britain and Holland. The 25,000 volt ac system gave promise of getting the work of electrification done much more cheaply.

Much attention has been given to the aesthetic appearance of locomotives and of the luxurious *grand-confort* coaches, so that now, with many trains covering long stretches of the Northern, Eastern and PLM lines at 100 mph, and the fastest trains on the former Orleans Railway running regularly at 125 mph, the trains themselves and their locomotives are more colourful than any in the long history of French railways. Steam traction is now virtually at an end, and on the lines not yet electrified the trains are hauled by handsomely styled diesel-electric locomotives.

Above left. French National Railways: *Le Capitole du Matin*—super-speed electric express train bound for Toulouse, at the Gare d'Austerlitz, Paris. Much of the run between Paris and Limoges is covered at 125 mph by these 8000 hp electric locomotives.
Below left. French National Railways: the *Stanislas* express from Paris, on arrival at Strasbourg. The electric locomotive of the '1500' class is one of the most advanced technical designs in the world, with automatic regulation of the controls to maintain a constant pre-selected speed.
Above. One of the high-speed ETG turbotrains of the Paris-Cherbourg service. Introduced in 1970, the trains are powered by a gas-turbine unit at one end and a diesel unit at the other.
Right. The prototype ultra-high speed gas-turbine train, which has attained a speed of 197 mph on tests south of Bordeaux.

41

Europe

Switzerland

In their mechanical, as distinct from their electrical features, the present success of modern non-steam locomotives in France can be traced back to an important Swiss development on the breathtakingly scenic Bern–Lötschberg–Simplon Railway, which in 1944 introduced an express electric locomotive which had all the wheels motor-driven. Hitherto on electric railways all over the world it had been thought essential to have non-powered leading and trailing wheels to provide adequate guiding influence, like the leading bogie of a steam locomotive. The new Lötschberg locomotives, carried on eight wheels, were a great success and the general principle of the mechanical design was adopted by the Swiss Federal Railways, and the authorities in France, to good effect.

On the great Alpine routes, the Gotthard, the Lötschberg and the Simplon, together with the metric-gauge lines traversed by a train like *The Glacier Express*, the Swiss railways offer one a glimpse of some of the finest scenery in the world. I use the word 'glimpse' with some deliberation, because it is often difficult from one train window to appreciate the full grandeur of the country.

The two preserved Rhaetian 2-8-0s together on a special train on the south side of the Albula Pass, towards Bevers in the Engadine.

There is a strong desire to dash from one side to the other! A front seat in one of the special 'Trans-Europ-Express' railcar trains gives a better impression, but best of all is that privileged place that I have several times had the pleasure of having, in the driver's cab. Then the bewildering spiral locations of the Gotthard 'ramps', the amazing descent of the Lötschberg line into the Rhône valley, and the alternations between rack and adhesion on the precipitous inclines of the Brünig Railway, between Interlaken and Lucerne, can be enjoyed to the utmost; they are unique.

It is some time since there was any regular steam working in Switzerland and one had to visit that most beautiful of transport museums on the lake shore at Lucerne to see what some of the principal types of locomotives were like. But in keen appreciation of the tourist value in steam hauled trips, the Swiss Federal Railways have restored to full working order one of the celebrated Series A3/5 4-6-0s that was originally intended to be no more than a static museum piece at Lucerne. This locomotive, No. 705, is of a design originating on the Jura–Simplon Railway and dating back to 1902. The class, which eventually numbered one hundred and eleven, were four-cylinder compounds on the de Glehn system, and No. 705 is probably the oldest working example of that system.

The Rhaetian Railway is the longest and most complex of all the Swiss metre gauge lines. It is well known for its breathtaking electric runs in the High Alps and trains like *The Glacier Express*, and has also not neglected to preserve two of its steam locomotives in full working order. Unlike the Swiss Federal Railways preserved examples, the Rhaetian 2-8-0s are two-cylinder simples and were built, like very many other Swiss engines, by the SLM Company at Winterthur, in the Rhaetian 2-8-0 case between 1906 and 1915.

Above left. One of the standard electric locomotives of the Rhaetian Railway at Cavadürli, on a train from Davos to Landquart.
Left. On the Swiss Federal Railways: the de Glehn four-cylinder compound 4-6-0 No. 705, of 1902 design, was originated by the Jura–Simplon Railway and used on the expresses on the Rhône Valley main line. It is here seen on a special train near Winterthur.
Above right. Rhaetian Railway: one of the two series G 4/5 2-8-0 locomotives now preserved, here seen on the turntable at Landquart. The design, which incorporates a four-wheeled tender, dates from 1906.
Right. On the metre gauge Rhaetian Railway: a rotary snow plough at Klosters, propelled by one of the two preserved 2-8-0 steam locomotives.

Europe
Austria

Below. A memory of Karl Gölsdorf and the nineteenth century: an ancient 2-6-0 tank engine, with the characteristic double-domed boiler, stands in Neuberg station on a train for Mürzzuschlag.
Right. A passenger train on the Eisenerz railway: one of the Gölsdorf 0-6-2 tank engines, propelling the 12.39 train from Vordernberg to Eisenerz, near Vordernberg Markt.

It is an easy transition from Switzerland into Austria, by the magnificent Arlberg Route, leading into the heart of the Tyrol. In the early years of the twentieth century Austrian steam locomotives were among the most colourful in Europe. But today the most picturesque of Karl Gölsdorf's creations are no more than museum pieces, and only a few of his earlier two-cylinder compounds, designed initially to haul passenger trains over the very severe gradients of the Arlberg route, remain in revenue earning service in Styria. While the student of modernized transport will admire the efficient way in which electric locomotives deal with the mountain gradients of the Tyrol, and of the Semmering Pass, through which the Austrian Southern Railway took the line that was once the main all-Austrian route from Vienna to Trieste, the romance of railways lies in the remaining pockets of steam, mostly on the narrow gauge.

At Jenbach, for example, on the main line westwards into the Tyrol, not one but *two* narrow-gauge lines start away into the mountains. Going north is the Achensee line climbing so steeply up the hillside as to need a rack rail, and coming to the bleak, tree-less lake that gives the railway its name. From the other side of the main line at Jenbach there strikes out the Zillertalbahn, through beautiful Tyrolean valley scenery running mostly at river level and worked by picturesque little steam locomotives. Perhaps the most fascinating of all the Austrian narrow-gauge steam railways are the true mountain climbers. There is the Schafberg, in the Salzkammergut district, easy of access from Salzburg, that starts from the village of St Wolfgang, immortalized in the operetta *White Horse Inn*, and climbs to the summit of the Schafberg, all the time overlooking the beautiful lake, the Wolfgangsee. Then, south of Vienna, from Püchberg, there is the railway climbing to the summit of the Schneeberg, a very busy little rack railway all the year round, on

which there are often five or six steam
locomotives in service simultaneously.

One of the most remarkable mountain
rack railways in the world is, however,
concerned no more than incidentally with
passenger tourist traffic. This is the iron-ore
carrying line up the Iron Mountain, in
Styria. The Eisenerz holds enormous deposits of iron ore, which are worked by opencast methods. There is no need for mining, as
such, and the railway was built in 1890 to
convey the ore down the side of the mountain,
on very steep gradients, and the rack system
of propulsion is used to obviate slipping. The
locomotives have gradually increased in
size from the 0-6-2 tank engines of 1900;
then came some 0-12-0s, designed by the
great Karl Gölsdorf, and finally two enormous 2-12-2s built during World War II,
when the Austrian railways were under
German control. The station of Prebichl
is at the summit of the climb from Donawitz.
The iron-ore workings are some distance
down the other side. So, the rack locomotives
are required not only for the down-grade
working of loaded trains but also for working
these trains *up* the steep incline from Eisenerz
to the summit of Prebichl. Also it certainly
would not be practicable to work iron-ore
empties up from Donawitz without the
rack, especially in winter, as the ruling
gradient is 1 in 15. The same applies to the
passenger services.

Above left. The fascination of the narrow gauge
in Austria: on the Steyertal line an 0-6-2 tank
engine No. 298-53 is shunting at Grunberg.
Below left. One of the tall and impressive 4-6-4
tank engines of Class '78' of 1931 vintage
stopping at Hieflau, in the course of a run from
Amstetten to Selztal.
Below. A diverting scene at St. Martin, on the
line from Gmünd to Grossgernungs: while the

0-8-0 engine No. 39903 rests and takes water,
the crew do the shunting — by muscle power!
Above. A remarkable rack railway in Styria: to
connect the opencast iron ore workings on the
Iron Mountain (Eisenerz) with the Vienna—
Villach main line a railway with gradients up to
1 in 14 was built. Here, on the rack section
between Vordernberg and Prebichl summit, a
Gölsdorf 0-6-2 hauls a load of hopper wagons.

Europe

Italy

The railways of Italy share with those of Belgium the reputation of having produced some of the most curiously shaped steam locomotives ever to run. The days of Signor Plancher's cab-in-front type of 4-6-0 have long passed. In some ways these were the forerunners of the gigantic cab-in-front articulated engines on the Southern Pacific in the USA; but the Italians being coal burners required the coal to be near at hand, and it was stacked in narrow and inconveniently shaped bunkers on either side of the footplate. Between the disappearance of Plancher's 'masterpieces' and the present time, rapid strides have been made towards the building up of a complete electric railway network; and as in France, all the earlier electric locomotives were dull to look at.

In the 'autumn' of steam working in Italy the vogue for the curious shape reappeared, not as a created style with the idea of attracting attention, but in the never-ending quest for improved thermal efficiency. An Italian engineer, Attilio Franco, had begun experiments to produce more efficient boilers in 1914; but the times were not propitious and it was not until 1932 that any result emerged, from a Belgian works at Nivelles. Then, in 1937, a Franco boiler was put on to one of the Plancher cab-in-front 4-6-0s, with good results. It was nevertheless something of a 'box-of-tricks', and the first truly practical exposition of the Franco boiler principles came from Piero Crosti. There were two subsidiary boilers slung pannier-wise along each side of the main boiler, and the steam and exhaust gas circuit was such that the chimney was not in its usual place but duplicated one half each at the near end of the subsidiary boilers. To the casual onlooker it seemed that engines with the Franco-Crosti boiler had no chimney at all. They were a great success and the Italians had many of them. Oddly enough Venice was one of their principal haunts, at a large depot by the station at the end of the causeway, from which one's taxi into the city is a gondola.

One of the numerous '640' class 2-6-0s which were unusual in having inside cylinders but outside Walschaert's valve gear. In this picture taken at Aosta engine No. 640.071 is specially turned out, with national flags for a special train working in 1972.

Never were beauty and mis-shapedness so violently contrasted as by the watercraft of Venice and the locomotives with the Franco-Crosti boiler!

One of the most interesting and distinctive among Italian steam locomotives in recent years were the 2-6-0s of 'Group 640'. These were express passenger engines for use on secondary routes that were laid with light rails, but were distinctive in having inside cylinders, though with the valve gear and the piston valves outside – an inversion of the normal order. They were fast and very sweet running machines, travelling in almost complete silence. Some of them were later rebuilt with the rotary cam type of valve gear invented by Arturo Caprotti, a mechanism that won considerable acceptance outside Italy and was used on a number of British and Indian locomotives.

Right. A Locomotive with the Franco-Crosti boiler
Above left. 2-6-0 No. 625.042 on a special from Salerno, in June 1974, pictured here at Lagonegro.
Below left. The GRAF special of June 1974 preparing to leave Salerno. It has the same 2-6-0, No. 625.042 as shown at Lagonegro, but is here assisted by a 2-8-0 No. 744.015.
Below. On the Sardinian Railways: a 2-6-2 narrow gauge tank engine No. 400, on a special train from Arbatax to Mandas at the station for Villanova Tulo.

Europe
Turkey

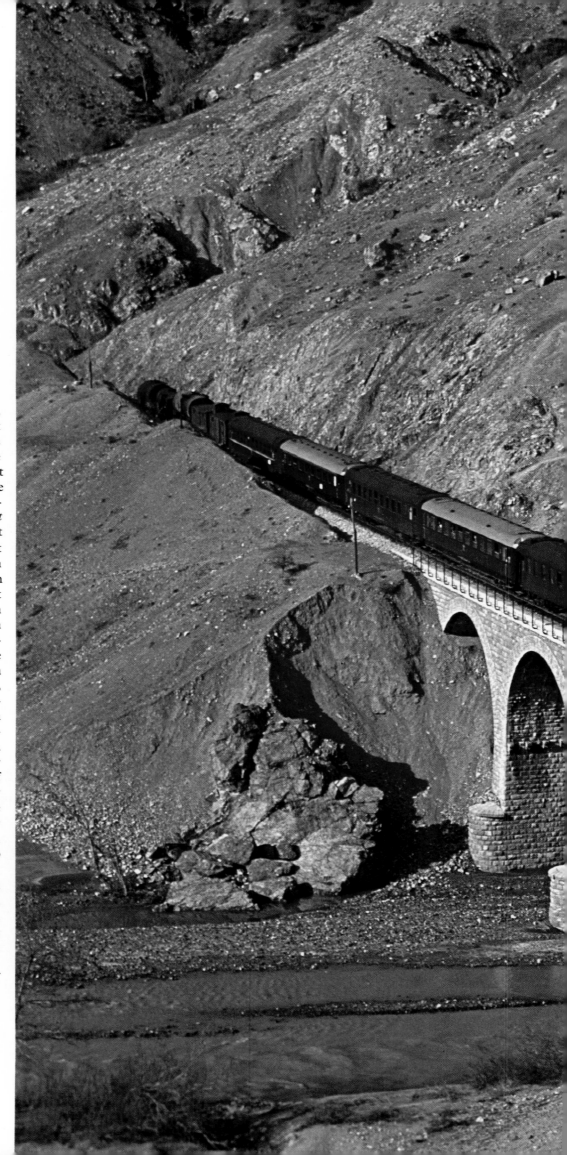

In no country of the world, perhaps, has political and economic development had such an effect upon railways as in Turkey. The old Ottoman Empire straddled the Bosphorus, and to most travellers of international experience Turkey meant no more than the easternmost sections on the long run of the *Orient Express*, from Paris to Constantinople, as it was then. But the Balkan War of 1913 left Turkey with no more than a foothold in Europe, and it is with the Turkish railways in Asia Minor that we are here concerned. At the outbreak of World War I there were in that territory about 2,500 miles of route in operation, mostly independent and unconnected and serving only the most fertile and prosperous areas. There had been a major though somewhat disjointed project, started in 1903, to build a through, standard-gauge line connecting Constantinople with Baghdad, and under strong German influence and finance this was pushed through to completion in 1918; but during the war the Turkish railways generally, starved of essential supplies and denuded of key labour, fell into a sorry state, and after the surrender a few old Great Western Railway 0-6-0 goods engines that had been used on the Salonica Front were transferred to help the system to keep going.

The emergence of the distinguished military commander Mustapha Kemal, afterwards so well known as Atatürk, as a strong and far-seeing national leader, and the subsequent proclamation of the Turkish Republic in October 1923, changed everything. The capital city and the seat of

Through passenger train from Kurtalan to Istanbul in rugged country between Ergani and Maden. The locomotive is one of the standard oil fired 2-10-0s of the TCDD, built between 1937 and 1949 by Henschel, in Germany, the Vulcan Foundry, and Skoda, in Czechoslovakia.

government was moved from Constantinople to the wholly Turkish but hitherto remote Ankara, then served by no more than a branch from Eskişehir, on the Baghdad railway, that made a meandering course towards the Mediterranean coast through Konya. A balanced system of railways was essential for the economic development of the country as a whole, and in 1927 the General Management of the Railways and Harbours of the Republic of Turkey (TCDD) was set up. Since then the railway mileage has been almost doubled in building up an integrated national system. Ankara, of course, was placed on the principal main lines leading to the Iraqi and Soviet Russian frontiers, though the route of the celebrated *Taurus Express*, from Istanbul to Baghdad, did not become any less important a line for that.

The countryside is everywhere extremely mountainous and, unless an altogether disproportionate expense had been in-

curred in colossal earthworks and long tunnels, the new lines had to be built following the winding river valleys and high mountain passes. The gradients in many places are very severe and this, together with the spectacular scenery, has provided the attraction for railway photographers and a challenge to their skills. The sight of a heavy train being hauled up a 1 in 40 gradient by two large 2-10-0 locomotives and pushed in the rear by a third is irresistible. Since the formation of TCDD most of the steam locomotives have been of German origin and manufacture, the earliest being direct developments of earlier standard Prussian State designs. In 1937, however, the famous firm of Henschel of Kassel delivered the first of a class of 2-10-0 mixed traffic locomotives that was destined to be international in its construction. Although the first 79 of a very successful design were built by Henschel, a further 37 were built in England after the war and delivered in

1948. A further 50 were supplied by Skoda, of Czechoslovakia, in 1949.

The period of World War II, and its aftermath, saw many locomotives of foreign origin drafted to the TCDD. Among these were the German *Kriegslok* 2-10-0, which proved very useful on some of the Turkish secondary lines where axle loads were limited. Then there were British 2-8-0s of the Stanier LMS '8F' class, and American 2-8-0s and 2-8-2s. Among locomotives built specially for service in Turkey some of the most spectacular are the enormous three-cylinder 2-10-2 tanks, for rear-end banking on the ten-mile long incline between Bilecik and Karakoy, on that part of the original main line from Istanbul to the Iraqi frontier that still remains the main route, after the later diversion of the section further east to pass through Ankara instead of through Konya. Four of these enormous engines were delivered from West Germany in 1951–2.

Below left. One of the American-built 2-10-0s making a spectacular start from Cankiri on a mixed train from Zonguldak to Irmak. The locomotives are mechanically stoked and the fireman was evidently making full use of his equipment when this photograph was taken.
Above left. One of the American-built Vulcan 2-10-0s in wild mountain country near Tuney on a freight from Zonguldak to Irmak.
Below. In the Taurus Mountains a mixed train from Adana is climbing towards Ulukisla. The locomotive is of the German '44' class 2-10-0, used in France during World War II, and one of 48 such locomotives bought from France in 1958.

Europe

Spain

Spain by tradition is one of the most colourful countries of Europe and until the protracted Civil War of 1936–9, the individual railway companies provided a picturesque if not very profitable echo of national characteristics. Reputedly influenced by Brunel's advocacy of a wider gauge than the standard 4ft 8½in adopted over the rest of Western Europe, Spain and inevitably Portugal, too, decided upon 5ft 6in, with consequent difficulties for traffic exchange at the international frontiers that have remained ever since, and which are now being no more than partially removed by the ingenious wheel-changing arrangements at Hendaye and Cerbère. The enthusiast travelling upon the Spanish railways will delight in the individualism in locomotive practice of the former independent railway companies evidenced by the many surviving units of the Northern, Western, Andalusian Central of Aragon, and the MZA (Madrid, Zaragoza and Alicante) organizations. Now, however, few steam locomotives remain in regular service on the national system.

It was in 1941, two years after the end of the Civil War, that RENFE (*Red Nacional de los Ferrocarriles Españoles*) was formed and a coordinated national policy for reconstruction and development was formulated. Something was certainly needed after the devastation left in certain areas by the Civil War, but the year 1941 was hardly a propitious time to put plans into execution, with nearly all the most likely sources of materials and rolling stock involved in vastly greater conflict than Spain had ever known. Fortunately much of the locomotive stock of the old railway companies was of sound design. The 4-8-0 had been a favourite type in Spain and impressive examples were to be seen on all the old lines. One of the most interesting and widely used was one introduced on the Andalusian railway in 1935. It was adopted soon after the end of the Civil War by both the Western and the MZA railways, and immediately accepted in 1941 as a RENFE standard. Construction continued down to the year 1953, by which time 247 engines of this class were at work.

The heavy gradients and difficult operating conditions in Spain that make things so exciting and colourful for the photographer have led to the designing of still larger engines than the popular 4-8-0s, and as early as 1925 the Northern introduced a class of 4-8-2s—65 of them in all—which at that time must have ranked among the heaviest and most powerful locomotives in Europe. Certainly the Northern, with its heavily graded lines running from Madrid to Gijón and Santander on the Atlantic coast, had a tough job, and these great locomotives worked passenger and freight trains alike. Most locomotives of the RENFE are plain black, albeit very smartly turned out; but this 240/4001 class was honoured by being lined in yellow.

Above. On the Miranda to Zaragoza line, Spain, one of the numerous and efficient 141F class 2-8-2s of which construction continued down to the year 1960, seen here in spectacular country near San Felices.
Below right. Amid grandly impressive mountain scenery one of the giant '242F' 4-8-4 locomotives of RENFE heads an express from Miranda to Zaragoza. These engines are the only ones on the Spanish National Railways to have the green livery.
Above right. Along the Ponferrada–Villablino line a local train is running placidly along hauled by a tender-tank locomotive No. 31, built by Maffei, of Munich, in 1913.

The ultimate in Spanish steam power was attained in 1935 with the production by the firm of Maquinista of the giant 4-8-4s of the 2001 class. These were designed for the Avila–Alsasua section of the Madrid–Irún main line, though their service on this duty did not last long. The extension of electric traction on this important international route curtailed their activities and when I was last in Spain in 1970 they were stationed at Miranda de Ebro, still beautifully turned out in the green livery that distinguishes them from all other locomotives of the RENFE.

Left. On the Ponferrada to Villablino line, in León, Spain, a freight train is crossing the fine viaduct near Santa Marina, hauled by an American built 2-6-2 tank engine of 1919 vintage, running bunker first.
Above. A British-built veteran of 1889 belonging formerly to the Great Southern Railway of Spain, on a goods train from Alcantarilla to Lorca. The twenty five engines of this class were built at intervals between 1889 and 1905, and all were named. The manufacturers were Neilsons, Kitsons, Sharp Stewart, and of the last six, in 1905, the North British Locomotive Company. They were very British in appearance until withdrawn from service.

Europe
Portugal

In Portugal the nationalized railway system was formed in 1947 with the combination of the virtually independent lines lying north and south of the Tagus estuary. The southern group, which was much the smaller, provided the service to the coast at Faro, while the north group included the principal internal main line between Lisbon and Oporto, and the lines carrying the international express trains, via Vilar Formoso, for the north and connections to Paris, via Marvão to Madrid and Barcelona, and via Elvas to Seville. But the enthusiast seeking the truly colourful side of Portuguese railroading will travel to the valley of the Douro in the north, and seek out the various narrow-gauge branches that strike off northwards from the Oporto–Barca de Alva main line where steam is still supreme.

To say that this area is a paradise for the railway enthusiast would be an understatement. There is the happy combination of beautiful country and narrow-gauge steam-operated branch lines. More than this, although this is now becoming a European outpost of steam, there is no evidence of the decay and dereliction that all too often has set in when the time was approaching for the inevitable change in motive power. The black steam locomotives with their polished copper tops to their shapely chimneys are kept in superb condition and provide ample evidence of how splendid a black locomotive can look if it is well cared for. Among individual locomotive types, the Mallet compound tanks are the most interesting. They were all built by Henschel of Kassel, Germany, but are uniformly of a very 'British' appearance. The older ones, dating from 1905, are of the 0-4-4-0 type but in 1911 the much larger variety was introduced having the rather extraordinary wheel arrangement 2-4-6-0. The first batch consisted of four only; but these proved very successful. Two more were purchased in 1913, and in 1923 a large repeat order for twelve more was placed with Henschel. It is worth going to the Douro Valley, if only to see these engines at work.

Amid the rugged scenery of the Douro Valley, a 4-6-0 No. 284 leaves a short tunnel near Tua, working an eastbound train.

Above. Compound 4-6-0 No. 238 with a mixed
load between Panserat and Vesuvio.
Above right. The morning mixed train to
Pochino, crossing the mouth of the river Tua,
where it enters the Douro. The train is hauled by a
2-8-4 tank engine.

Below right. On the 5ft 6in gauge main line up the valley of the Douro, North Portugal, an inside cylinder 4-6-0 No. 285 makes a vigorous start out of Pinhao with an early morning freight to Barca de Alva, on the Spanish frontier.

Left. Two of the Mallet 2-4-6-0 compound tank engines at Sernada-de-Vluga: No. 182 leaving on a train to Viseu; No. 215 shunting.
Below. The morning train from Oporto to Fafe leaves Lousado, behind engine No. 166. An equally resplendent 102 is on the shed.
Bottom. On shed at Nine, Portugal, a Henschel built 2-6-4 tank locomotive, No. 87 of 1929 vintage.

Top. Massed locomotive power in a round-house provides an impressive and colourful sight, especially when the locomotives on shed are so splendidly clean as here, at Contumil shed, Oporto, Portugal.

Above. On the standard gauge in Portugal: a Pacific No. 560 on a goods train from Monção to Viana, near Ancora.

Right. One of the remarkable 2-4-6-0 Mallet compound tank engines, speeds on the Corgo line. These metre gauge locomotives provide one of the few examples of a Mallet compound on which the number of coupled wheels on the forward and rear engine is not the same.

Europe
Scandinavia

Below. A Swedish 2-6-4 tank No. 1306 running a special train from Ludvika to Fagersta, amid beautiful and characteristic lake country.

Above and far left. The Finnish State Railways operate under extremely severe weather conditions in winter. Certain freight trains, as these between Kemi and Kemi Harbour, are run only when the Baltic Sea is frozen over and extra traffic has to be taken by rail. In both these photographs the locomotive is TR3 2-8-0 No. 1153, a wood-burner, with the special spark arresting chimney.
Left. In contrasting beautiful summer weather a Finnish 'Pacific' No. 1001 leaves Riihimaki on an evening train for Tampere.

Indian spectacular

I cannot think of a more interesting day excursion than the one from Delhi to Agra, and none but the keenest and one-track-minded rail buff would go to Agra and not see something of the marvellous array of monuments within easy distance of the city centre. To work the *Taj Express* is a prestige job for the locomotive department, and the big semi-streamlined Pacific of the 'WP' class is resplendent in black and pale green. The green indicates Central Railway, and is symbolic of the more colourful era now existing on the Indian railways. To appreciate its significance one has to take the history of railways in India back roughly 100 years, when the present network was being built up. Then, although there were a considerable number of apparently independent companies, some with their head offices in London, the prospect of eventual takeover by the State hung over them all. The contracts they held were for a limited number of years only, and by the latter part of the nineteenth century quite a number were wholly State-owned and managed, though retaining names appropriate to the territorial activities.

Long before the Indian Empire gave place to the Dominion of India, and then to the Republic, the majority of the railways had passed into State control, though there remained the former individual features of great lines like the East Indian, the Great Indian Peninsula, and the Bombay, Baroda and Central India, together with their distinctive locomotive and carriage liveries. With the granting of independence in 1947, and the establishment also of the states of West and East Pakistan, some of the former railways, notably the North Western and the Bengal and Assam, found their main routes severed, and drastic revision of their activities became necessary. Of the great and efficient North Western Railway only the lines southeast of Amritsar remained in India, and in due course some

regrouping of administrative areas was necessary, to set up regional territories of approximately equal business extent, though not necessarily of equal mileage, or ownership of rolling stock. Some of the new 'railways' approximated to the older 'companies'. For example, the 'Central' covered most of the area formerly worked by the Great Indian Peninsula; the 'Western' took over the B.B. & C.I, while the South Eastern took that of the Bengal-Nagpur.

While a huge programme of standardization of locomotives, to cover requirements of all India, was set in motion, aiming to have the minimum number of separate classes, distinctive colours were adopted by the different railways, and passenger engines of all vintages, and some freight also, were finished in two-tone colourschemes, with black as the unifying tone. Thus one finds leaf green as the second tone on Central Railway engines, orange for the Southern, red-brown for the Northern, and blue-green for the Eastern – to mention only a few. The bullet-nosed smokebox fronts of the 'WP' Pacifics, as exemplified by the engine of the *Taj Express*, are embellished with ornamental stars, the points sometimes alternating between colour and stainless steel. Then take a look inside the cab of the 'Taj' engine: the various fittings gleam like the contents of a jeweler's shop, and over the firehole door is a beautiful silhouette of the Taj Mahal itself, worked with all the skill of the Indian craftsman in brasswork. I rode most of the way to Agra on the footplate and once we started, and worked up to a steady 60 mph, that decorative engine reverted to the commonplace; she rattled and banged along just like any other hard-worked unit and devoured all the coal that two young firemen, shovelling in turn, could get through the firedoor.

The Indian railways started before political control of the subcontinent passed to the Crown in 1858, and before it had achieved its later Imperial status, and it was

when administration was in the hands of the East India Company that the great Governor-General, the Marquis of Dalhousie, drew up the scheme of main routes which is still the backbone of the Indian railways today. He went to India straight from an important post at the Board of Trade, in England, and had been so involved in all the controversy over railway gauges, following Brunel's adoption of 7 ft for the Great Western, that he laid down emphatically that in India there must be only one gauge. The starting points of the pioneer Indian railways were originally very far from each other – in Bombay, in Calcutta, and in Madras; but the plan he drew up envisaged a connected and integral network, and a standard rail gauge of 5 ft 6 in was laid down.

As the master plan took shape, however, it was apparent that to take full advantage of railway transport many feeder lines would be needed. There were times of famine and distress that could be relieved only by effective transport, and yet there was little prospect of major 5ft 6 in gauge lines in such areas paying their way. Thus was conceived the idea of having a subsidiary network of feeder lines built on the metre gauge. Some were entirely new railway systems, like the Southern Mahratta and the Assam–Bengal; there were metre-gauge branches built within existing companies, of which the network west of the Bombay, Baroda and Central India broad-gauge main line was one of the notable examples, and there was an extensive mileage built up in the southernmost part of India. The Burma railways, separated from those of India by the intervening mountain ranges were built entirely on the metre gauge. For the lighter traffic and slower speeds many picturesque locomotives were built specially, and as many of them survive today they are much sought after by photographers, who travel far off the beaten track of tourists in India to find these old locomotives still at work.

Top right. A 2ft 6in gauge 0-6-2 tender engine built by Bagnall of Stafford in 1912 in service at Bhavnagar in December 1974.
Centre right. Another Bagnall narrow gauge, a tank engine, of 1926, 0-6-4 'WT' class in service on the Western Railway.
Right. A highly decorated 2ft 6in gauge 0-6-2 'W' class built 1913, and in service at Nadiad, Western Railway in 1974.
Left. One of the finely embellished 'WP' streamlined 4-6-2s of the Central Railway passing Delhi Junction with an express for the south.

Not surprisingly, traffic conditions in many parts of India have changed considerably in the 100 years since the Viceroyalty of Lord Mayo, when construction on the metre gauge was first authorized. The changes are nowhere more evident than in the far south, in the populous state of Kerala, and there at least one section of a line built on the metre gauge has been converted to the broad 5 ft 6 in gauge, between Ernakulam and Trivandrum. Travelling on this line, seeing the works in progress, and the continuous forests of palm trees that make the countryside look like a vast impenetrable jungle, it was hard to realize that this is the most densely populated part of India. There may be intense concentrations in the great cities of the north, but between them in the valley of the Ganga, for example, the countryside is entirely rural for hundreds of miles. Not so in Kerala, where the villages follow thick and fast, and every country station has its crowd of gaily attired passengers waiting for the train. In recent years new and powerful locomotives have been designed specially for the metre gauge and in their various operating areas they carry the colours of their regions.

The electric suburban trains of Bombay and Calcutta have a colour and character that is unique among commuter services around great cities. It is not so much the trains themselves, although the working observed from one or another of the modern efficiently controlled push-button-panel signal boxes is impressive enough, it is the passengers who provide most of the colour. One does not fully appreciate what crowding means on a railway train until going to Howrah or Sealdah in Calcutta, or to Churchgate or Victoria Terminus in Bombay. The fast electric suburban trains have sliding doors, but nobody ever attempts to close them. During the day they are left open to keep the carriages cool inside, and in the rush-hour peaks the trains are so jampacked inside that there is a bunch of passengers hanging on around the doors. The trains present an extraordinary sight with these clusters, two to every carriage all along the lengthy trains. Most of these intrepid commuters are clad in white, but at the doors of the 'Ladies Only' carriages there are equally animated clusters, in saris of every colour in the rainbow, with draperies flying in the wind as the trains sweep along at anything up to 50 mph.

To see Indian commuting at its most intense one needs to be at Howrah on the right bank of the Hooghly River, about

A colourful Indian Railway scene at Danapur, with a 'WG' class standard 2-8-2, and passengers, squatters and others disporting themselves on the track.

10 am, when three of these packed trains come into the terminus simultaneously and together discharge between *nine and ten thousand* people into the station concourse within seconds of each other! The railway operation is as smart and efficient as in any London station. These multiple-unit electric trains are never at the platforms for more than about six or seven minutes. They go out either as empty stock, to await the needs of the outgoing suburban rush, or provide an outward passenger service. There is no time to spare, for the platform space is needed for the next inward-bound train, bringing another 3,000 passengers.

In complete contrast are the 'hill' railways of India, on the narrow gauge. As British administration developed, from the early days of the East India Company to the Imperial epoch of the latter part of the nineteenth century, the seat of Government was transferred in the hot season from Calcutta to the hill stations of the Himalayas, and two spectacular little railways were built climbing high into the mountains. The first of these mounted from Siliguri, north of Calcutta, to the romantically situated mountain resort of Darjeeling. It was built in 1879–81, on the 2 ft gauge, and at the time was considered quite an incredible feat of railway engineering. Today it could be regarded as a top tourist attraction, but still more remarkable is the fact that it remains steam-worked, and by a type of saddle-tank locomotive first introduced in 1889!

The engineer who surveyed and built this railway resorted to every known device to gain height, because a summit level of 7,407 ft above sea level, at Ghum, was unavoidable. He used spiral locations, 'Z' type reversing stations and long gradients of 1 in 25, with sections as steep as 1 in 20; but unlike the mountain railways of Europe there were no rack sections. And up from the jungle lands of Siliguri, round the bewildering spirals, the little trains pound along, with two men riding on the buffer beam to put sand on the rails to check any slipping. The track climbs high above the jungle and the cloud level into the clear blue sky, where there are breathtaking views of the eternal snows of the main Himalayan range. As traffic developed and the line prospered, more and more of the little 0-4-0 saddle-tank engines were bought, all of identical design, until by 1927 there were no fewer than 34 of them in service. It is no wonder that railway enthusiasts from all over the world make the long and not easy journey to Siliguri, to ride up to Darjeeling.

When the summer seat of the Imperial Government was established at Simla, in the northern mountain regions of the Punjab, work on a narrow-gauge railway from Kalka was started in 1899 and completed in 1903 on the broad-gauge network of the former North Western Railway. The respective altitudes of Kalka and Simla are 2,154 and 6,819 ft and 'as the crow flies' the distance is only 30 miles. But the intervening distance includes some of the most jumbled and erratic mountain wilderness one could possibly imagine. It is badly affected by landslides and subsidences during the monsoon season, and to get anything like a stable track the engineers had to take a very meandering course round the hillsides, to such an extent that the distance by the railway from Kalka to Simla is no less than 60 miles. There are no reversing stations, and no spirals – just one continuous hard grind. Today the line is worked by diesel power; but some of the 'K' class 2-6-2 tank engines were still at Kalka when I was there in January 1975. In the days of the North Western Railway they were painted black, but those remaining were finished in the standard style of the Northern Railway, with the side tanks half black, and half red-brown.

Quite distinct from these two railways leading into the foothills of the Himalayas, but equally fascinating, is the narrow-gauge line from Mettuppalaiyam to Ootacamund in the Nilgiri Hills, in south India, usually known as the Ooty Line. This is unique in India in that the traction is partly adhesion and partly by rack, on the principle developed for certain through routes in Switzerland, where gradients of exceptional severity are encountered in the course of a journey that can be worked by adhesion over much of the total mileage. The distance by rail is $28\frac{3}{4}$ miles and the difference in altitude is from 1,071 ft at Mettupalaiyam to 7,228 ft at Ootacamund. The rack sections are inclined at 1 in $12\frac{1}{2}$, and the adhesion stretches 1 in 25 – which is steep enough!

The powerful steam locomotives of the 'X' class, introduced from 1914 onwards, were built in Switzerland and include the same principle of operation as those formerly used on the Brünig railway. They are of the 0-8-2 tank type, four-cylinder compounds, with all four cylinders outside. The high-pressure cylinders drive the ordinary 'road' wheels, and when working adhesion only the engine operates as a two-cylinder simple. On the rack sections working is changed over to compound and the low-pressure cylinders drive the rack pinions. The machinery looks very impressive in operation, when seen from the lineside, with a great proliferation of rods, wheels, cranks and rocking shafts all in rapid actuation. The locomotives are painted in a handsome blue livery, of a basic colour like that of the Caledonian Railway of Scotland. The scale is much larger than that of the 'hill' railways in the north, with metre-gauge track, and these locomotives weigh no less than 48 tons. On the upward journey to 'Ooty' the locomotives push their trains from the rear.

Above. A 'WL' class Pacific of the Southern Railway of India leaving Mettuppalaiyam on the 7.45 a.m. train to Coimbatore.
Above right. A passenger train passing Delhi Junction, hauled by a standard 2-8-2 'WG' class, with decorated smokebox.
Right. The Matheran Hill Railway is one of the most accessible of the hill railways of India, starting from Neral, on the main Bombay–Poona line. A little 0-6-0 tank engine of 1905 vintage, built by Orenstein & Koppel, of Berlin, toils up the 1 in 20 gradient.

The United States past and present

In no country of the world was the superseding of steam more rapid or more ruthless than in the USA. At the end of World War II the diesels swept in everywhere, and large numbers of powerful steam locomotives with a great deal of service still left in them were scrapped. The diesels, the majority of which were at first of General Motors standard design, were painted in bright, distinctive, and often garish colours; their goings and comings lacked the tremendous atmosphere of steam, particularly because in the USA heavy working on mountain gradients was frequently accompanied by highly spectacular exhausts of black smoke. The great locomotives of the New York Central, the Milwaukee Road, the Norfolk and Western and the Union Pacific – to mention only four – were in a long and distinguished line of descent from some of the most colourful engines that have ever run the rails, any-

where in the world. Not even in Great Britain, in the spacious days of the nineteenth century, were locomotives so gaily and fancifully adorned as the early American 4-4-0s. Although running in a wealth of different styles and a great diversity of colouring, the 4-4-0 with outside cylinders, a huge closed-in cab, and very often a colossal 'balloon' stack designed as a spark arrester, was so generally typical and so universal as to be called the American type.

While the slaughter of more modern locomotives was in progress before the advancing diesels, it was fortunate that a number of those old warriors was preserved, some in good enough condition still to be safely steamed. None of them surely appeared in more spectacular guise than old '144' of the Canadian Pacific, which steamed so many miles in Canada during the filming of the television serial *The National Dream*.

In the USA itself, one of the most

historic events in the history of railways is now commemorated out in the high country at Promontory, Utah, where the gangs building the first transcontinental line across America, working from east to west, met on 10 May 1869, and the last spike was one of gold. The section of line has actually been superseded by a diversion having an improved location, and the opportunity has been taken to erect the most fascinating memorial, with two locomotives representing the converging construction gangs of the Central Pacific and the Union Pacific Railroads, which came cowcatcher to cowcatcher at the driving of the last spike.

From this dramatic start the Union Pacific developed into one of the greatest of American railways. It came to possess, in the famous 4-8-8-4 'Big Boys' of 1942 the largest and heaviest steam locomotives ever built, and now it has some of the largest-ever diesel electrics. Its route through to the

West over the Wyoming hills is actually one of the easiest so far as gradients are concerned, though Sherman Hill provided tough enough going for the big 4-8-4 passenger locomotives to need double-heading with maximum-load trains. The modern steam locomotives of the Union Pacific, like those of most other American railways, were painted plain black and were an impressive sight blasting up Sherman Hill or bringing up great express freight trains from the west through the stark, rocky wilderness of Echo Canyon, Utah.

The Union Pacific 'Big Boys' were of the 'simple' Mallet articulated type, which was to North America what the Beyer–Garratt has been to the countries of the British Commonwealth. The true Mallet was a compound, with the low pressure cylinders driving the leading engine unit; but in later years most articulated locomotives of the basic Mallet form of construction were 'simples'. Mallets consisted of two separate engines beneath one colossal boiler. The rearward engine was carried on the main frames, while the forward one was on a truck that could swing from side to side, and thus give a degree of road flexibility to what would otherwise have been a very long locomotive. The Garratt, on the other hand, had the engine units fore and aft, and the boiler carried on a central cradle, forming a three-piece articulation. In America the Mallet was originally a slow-speed, heavy freight and mineral hauler. Supporting of the front part of the boiler on the articulated front engine unit was not a very certain job, and when the speed reached around 30 mph the riding became very rough, if not actually dangerous. This instability did not

Far left. Ancient and modern, side by side on the Atchison, Topeka and Santa Fe: a preserved Consolidation 2-8-0, with balloon-type smoke-stack, alongside one of the latest diesel-electric locomotives.
Above. A beautifully restored example of the 4-4-0 type, outside the Mount Clare Works of the Baltimore and Ohio Railroad, Baltimore, and named *William Mason*, after one of the most celebrated U.S. locomotive builders of the mid-nineteenth century.
Left. May 10, 1969 was the Centenary of the famous Golden Spike ceremony at Promontory, Utah, where the construction gangs of the Union Pacific working westwards, and of the Central Pacific working east met, and the last spike in the first transcontinental railway across America was driven in. Although the present main line does not now run over this location, the Centenary was marked by the creation of a National Memorial, in which a length of track was relaid, and two vintage locomotives were restored and repainted to represent the *Jupiter* of the Central Pacific, in the foreground, and the '119' of the Union Pacific, facing it. The ensemble together with a small exhibition building forms one of the most original kinds of railway museum to be found anywhere in the world.

matter so long as Mallet locomotives were used for toiling along at 10–15 mph with endless trains of coal or iron ore.

But on the Union Pacific in particular something considerably larger than the conventional 4-8-4s and 4-12-2s was needed for the fast freight and express fruit trains, and much study was given to the methods of supporting the front part of the boiler of these articulated locos and equalization of the weight carried on the front and rear engines. As a result of this research a simple 'articulated' with the 4-6-6-4 wheel arrangement was designed for the Union Pacific, which was not only an extremely powerful locomotive, but which was quite steady at speeds of more than 60 mph. They were indeed used on passenger trains up to speeds of about 80 mph. The experience gained with this type led to a series of notable express freight 'simple' Mallets being introduced on a number of American railways, notably the Denver and Rio Grande Western, on the Norfolk and Western, and on the Chesapeake and Ohio. The Norfolk and Western retained the 2-8-8-2 type with compound expansion for its heaviest mineral hauls. None of these locomotives was, however, as enormous as the Union Pacific 4-8-8-4 'Big Boys'.

For the heaviest express passenger service on routes that included hill climbing as well as much fast level running the 4-8-4 type represented the climax of American steam. Again the Union Pacific had a splendid design, which is shown in the picture on page 81, while on the neighbouring Denver and Rio Grande Western, cutting through some of the most rugged mountain country in the whole of North America, even large 4-8-4s were not enough to handle the heaviest trains without an assistant engine. Both routes west from Denver, that through the Moffatt Tunnel, and the highly spectacular Royal Gorge farther to the south, provided some of the most colourful railroading imaginable.

Still farther south, the Santa Fe set its final series of 4-8-4s some of the greatest feats of endurance, combined with maximum sustained demands for power, ever attempted with steam traction. On the very heavy sleeping-car expresses from Chicago to Los Angeles these great engines worked throughout over the 1,234 miles between La Junta, Colorado, and Los Angeles, being manned successively by *nine* different engine crews. These engines were oil-fired. In the eastern states the changeover to diesels did not come quite so rapidly. The coalfields were near at hand, and on the New York Central in particular engines of the new 'Niagara' class, 4-8-4s introduced at the close of World War II, were tested rigorously against diesels to compare running costs, fuel consumption and availability. It was always claimed that diesels did not require so much time between trips for servicing as did a steam locomotive. The

New York Central did not immediately accept this and considered that with a well-designed modern steam locomotive equally good figures for availability could be achieved. Although the first cost of a diesel was more than double that of a 'Niagara', the diesels showed up to advantage; but ultimately other factors intervened and the diesels took over on the New York Central as everywhere else.

One of the great problems with very long locomotives like the various articulated types was that of steam beating down and obscuring the driver's view ahead. The chimneys were so small and the boilers so large that except when blasting up heavy gradients, with the exhaust going sky-high, smoke and steam tended to cling to the surface of the boiler. On routes with lengthy tunnels often with no more than a

single-track bore, conditions in the driver's cab could become unpleasant, and there was sometimes even the danger of asphyxiation. On the Southern Pacific operating the important north-to-south route from Portland through San Francisco to Los Angeles, the largest locomotives were all oil-fired and as there was no need to have immediate access to the fuel, they turned their Mallet articulated engines back to front, as it were, having the driver's cab at the leading end and trailing the tender containing the oil and water supply behind what, in a normal locomotive, was the leading end. This not only gave the enginemen a clear lookout, but also put them well ahead of the exhaust steam when passing through the many tunnels on the route through the Sierras over Donner Pass.

The problem of smoke beating down was a troublesome one on American railways even before the nineteenth century was out, and it was solved on some of the eastern lines by putting the driver in a cab by himself, halfway along the boiler. Very quaint these engines looked, and as the

driver had to walk along to the 'cupboard' on the boiler, they earned the nickname of 'Mother Hubbards'. There was, on some railways, an even more cogent reason for doing this. The use of soft coal, or even of lignite, necessitated very large and wide fire boxes and it would have been difficult to fit a conventional cab within the limits of overall width. In another respect they must have been awkward engines to manage. The efficient operation of a steam locomotive requires close cooperation between driver and fireman, and on a 'Mother Hubbard' this cannot have been easy with the fireman on his own at the rear end. Nevertheless, engines of this type were used for some years on some of the fastest trains in America, the *Atlantic City Flyers* of the Philadelphia and Reading Railroad, between Philadelphia and Atlantic City.

The engines on these trains had the 4-4-2 wheel arrangement and because of this high-speed assignment the type became universally known as the 'Atlantic'. Loads were increasing to such an extent in the USA that larger engines were needed with six, and then eight, coupled wheels and in the country of its birth the 'Atlantic' type was not long in vogue. But it was widely adopted in Great Britain and France, and through the British influence its use became extensive also in India. Some of the most powerful American 'Atlantics' were developed on the Pennsylvania Railroad. The first of these were also built as 'Mother

Above. Norfolk and Western: one of the enormous Class Y6b Mallet compound 2-8-8-2s on a westbound empty coal train in the New River Gorge.
Right. Union Pacific Railroad: a special excursion leaving Denver, hauled by steam 4-8-4 locomotive No. 8444, with diesel-electrics following.

Hubbards'; but it was the 'E6' class – rather stumpy, and not very elegant to look upon – that had nevertheless a distinguished record of performance. When the very fast *Detroit Arrow* was put on in the early 1930s, at first with a light load, the train was worked by 'E6' Atlantics in preference to the much more powerful 'K4' Pacifics used on all other Pennsylvania express passenger services.

It was not until the 1940s that the Pennsylvania built anything larger than 'Pacifics' for its numerous, heavy, and very fast express trains. Except in crossing the Allegheny Mountains, between Pittsburgh and Harrisburg, the gradients east of Chicago and St Louis were easy and the need was for sustained high steaming at speeds of 75–85 mph. The great rival of the Pennsylvania, particularly on the prestige first-class service between New York and Chicago, was the New York Central and this line developed the 4-6-4 type, which provided the greater carrying capacity of a four-wheel truck beneath the huge fireboxes needed. The NYC trains, like the *Empire State Express* and the *Twentieth Century Limited*, often loaded to more than 1,000 tons – more than double that of the *Flying Scotsman* – and speeds in excess of 80 mph on level track were a daily requirement. At times of the heaviest traffic the 'Century' as it was always known, sometimes ran in three or four sections. It is sad to think that nowadays passenger traffic by rail in the USA has dwindled to such an extent that there is no through service from New York to Chicago by the former NYC route. Only the *Broadway Limited*, following the former Pennsylvania route, provides a fast overnight service between the two cities. In their day, the 4-6-4s of the New York Central were among the finest express passenger locomotives in North America.

Heading once more towards the mountains, it is interesting to recall that the Denver and Rio Grande Western, which today provides an important link in the east–west chain of communication across the USA, began its existence as a narrow-gauge line. In the first place it was not conceived as an east–west route at all. The 'Western' in its name was added later. The original plan was for a narrow-gauge line from Denver to the Rio Grande in the far south, which forms the international frontier between the USA and Mexico. But the railway from Denver never got anywhere near the Rio Grande. Instead, discovery of mineral wealth in the Colorado Rockies led to branches being built westward into the mountains, all on the narrow gauge; and in those fastnesses there took place some of the most exciting railway operations imaginable. Much of the original narrow-gauge mileage is now closed, but happily some sections have been preserved as tourist and railway enthusiast attractions, and visits to them are extremely popular. The summer service

over the 45¼ miles from Durango to Silverton features in the *Official Railway Guide* for North America, and is operated by the Denver and Rio Grande Western Railroad itself; but part of the section east of Durango, over the Cumbres Pass, is operated by the Cumbres and Toltec Scenic Railroad under a leasing arrangement with the states of New Mexico and Colorado.

The old main line to the west, which began with its junction with the standard gauge at Salida, went over the Continental Divide at the Marshall Pass, on through Gunnison and then over Cerro Summit with its fearsome curves and gradients of 1 in 25, is now closed; but the tales told of old-time operation on that line still linger in the Colorado Rockies. There were speed restrictions, it is true; but when a cargo was needed in a hurry, livestock for example, it was no unusual thing for a driver definitely to be instructed to disregard them all and get through as quickly as he could. Most of

the drivers needed little encouragement, and tales are told by some of the conductors (guards in British Railway parlance), that one could tell by the look in the eye of one old Boomer that 'he was gonna run like hell'. From this one must not imagine that the *actual* speeds were very high by ordinary railway standards; it is just that they were breathtaking on such a track and in such a terrain. A record run made in 1894 with a stock train over the 80 miles from Ridgeway

Above left. Denver and Rio Grande Western: an astonishing location on the narrow gauge line descending eastbound from the Cumbres Pass, Colorado. This 70-car freight train is so strung out round a bend that the 2-8-2 locomotive was photographed from the caboose of its own train!
Below left. Silverton, Colorado, a station on the same line.

Top. The glamour and colour of the vintage 2-8-0, No. 40, makes a perfect period picture on the narrow gauge in Colorado, at Central City.
Above. Along the track of the Denver and Rio Grande Western a pair of ex-Rio Grande narrow gauge 2-8-2s make ready with an excursion train for Antonita at Chama, New Mexico.

Above. Chicago, Milwaukee, St. Paul and Pacific: a westbound local train pulling out of the old Milwaukee station, Chicago, in 1952, hauled by Pacific locomotive No. 196.
Right. New York Central: the *Empire State Express* eastbound from Chicago to New York leaving Dunkirk N.Y. hauled by one of the celebrated J-3-a Hudson class 4-6-4 locomotives.
Far right. Chicago, Milwaukee, St. Paul and Pacific Railroad: in 1952, Pacific No. 165 leaving Chicago with a semi-fast passenger train.

to Gunnison gave an average speed of 18 mph. Today the Silverton passenger train takes $3\frac{1}{2}$ hours for the $45\frac{1}{4}$ miles from Durango.

Both on this line and on the Cumbres scenic line the locomotives are of 2-8-2 type of relatively modern design, and although operating on the 3 ft gauge they are very heavy and powerful units—not in comparison with the latest standard-gauge steam locomotives in America, but certainly in relation to those elsewhere in the world. They were introduced in 1923–5 and took over the hardest duties from an assortment of very picturesque old warriors. But even these new engines, which weigh as much as a 'Royal Scot', could not manage loads of more than 230 tons on the gradients of the Marshall Pass; and since the traffic people had to work 600-ton trains at times it needed three of the latest engines, two in front and one pushing in rear.

With very few exceptions American steam locomotives were painted plain black. Towards the end of the 1930s, when the first high-speed diesel railcar trains were being introduced, a few selected steam locomotives were streamlined, more for publicity effect than anything else, and some were painted in startling colours. The Chicago Milwaukee St Paul and Pacific, for example, put on the spectacular *Hiawatha* trains between Chicago and Milwaukee, which had to run at 100 mph in everyday service. Special high-speed engines were built and these had the silver-coloured streamlined casings adorned with orange and crimson bands. The New York Central was more restrained in the streamlined 4-6-4s put on to the *Twentieth Century Limited*, but the Southern Pacific went very gay with the semi-streamlined 4-8-4s built for the *Daylight Expresses*, between Los Angeles and San Francisco, having broad red and orange bands below the centre line of the boiler. Everything above that was black, except that the conical smokebox front was painted aluminium colour.

However, when the general introduction of diesel-electric locomotives began after World War II, the railways of America took on an entirely new look. In steam days when nearly everything was black one could just recognize some of the more distinctive of the company locomotives by their silhouettes; but the great majority of what we now call the 'first generation' diesels came from one manufacturer, General Motors, at their great plant at La Grange, Illinois. It was no accident that they all looked alike. The overriding policy of the firm was to sell a standard product and no other. The story is told of one railway administration wishing to buy a large batch of diesel-electric locomotives, but requiring certain deviations from the standard General Motors product to suit their own circumstances. The manufacturer stood rock solid. It was 'standard or nothing' and they refused to take the order! In one respect, however, General Motors did make a concession. They did not take the line of one English railway manager, who once said he did not mind what colour the locomotives were painted as long as it was black; and so, on the new diesels, the railways of America suddenly became strikingly distinguishable from each other by the adoption of gay new colour schemes. Some indeed went to the extent of having different colours for the freight and passenger locomotives.

The diesel revolution on the American railways was of course greatly regretted by all lovers of the steam locomotive, and there were business interests who felt that strict technological and economic factors were not considered with the impartiality necessary in the making of so important a

transition. But apart from anything else the diesels had an overwhelming advantage over steam. Locomotives of each kind might have an equal hauling capacity with a fast train at 60–80 mph on level track or easy gradients; but get into the mountains, and there are plenty of very severe inclines in North America, and at below 20 mph the diesel will have twice the tractive power of the otherwise equivalent steam locomotive. It was because of this that when the Canadian Pacific first introduced diesels they put them on to the divisions in the Rocky Mountains, where the climbing speed of both passenger and freight trains was usually no more than about 20 mph, not on the fast stretches across the open prairies. The other factor is of course the capacity for doubling up the power at the head-end without the need for

additional engine crews. Two, three or as many as five locomotives can be coupled together and through the electrical controls operated by one man and his co-driver. On the Canadian Pacific, for example, on the Beaver Hill, British Columbia, in steam days, the heaviest westbound trains needed four locomotives, each with its own crew. Now anything up to *nine* diesel-electric locomotives are controlled at the same time by two men only.

The decline in railway business, which has affected so many countries all over the world, has been especially severe in the USA, and although there has always been strong resistance to anything savouring of nationalization, it has been necessary to provide substantial support recently in the form of Federal funds. In 1970, by Act of

Congress, the National Railroad Passenger Corporation was set up to support the operation of a basic network of inter-city passenger trains. The routes chosen for operation under the auspices of AMTRAK were aimed to eliminate the duplication of service and competitive lines which, admirable in an era of boom demand, had led to the near-bankruptcy of certain of the individual railway companies. It is under this regrouping, for example, that the Pennsylvania route between New York and Chicago was chosen for support, with the *Broadway Limited* running now under AMTRAK colours.

As appropriate to the new set-up, so far as the principal passenger services are concerned, the locomotives and coaching stock on AMTRAK-sponsored trains are now painted in distinctive colours. The new style in grey, blue and red on the diesel locomotives is most attractive but it is imposing a degree of nationwide standardization whereby, for example, the *San Francisco Zephyr*, the *Hiawathas* of the Milwaukee Road, and the *Empire State Express*, run in the same colours as the Coast Daylight/Starlight, from Seattle to Los Angeles, or 'The Broadway Limited'. But it is better to have trains with a standardized colourscheme than no trains at all; and that catastrophe could easily have happened in the USA!

Below left. A dramatic location on the Union Pacific main line to the west: Weber Canyon, Utah. One of the largest ever diesels, No. 6929, of 6600 horsepower, coupled to *three more* diesels hauling a maximum tonnage freight train.

Below left. A dramatic location on the Union Pacific main line to the west: Weber Canyon, *Below.* Denver and Rio Grande Western: This is one of the routes not included in the Amtrak network, and the splendid train *Rio Grande Zephyr* is powered by locomotives in the railroad's own colours rather than those of Amtrak. The photograph is taken at Grand Junction, Colorado, where the two routes westward through the mountains link up.
Bottom. The 'Amtrak look': the *San Joaquin* express takes the Southern Pacific inland route from Los Angeles, serving San Francisco and continuing north to Seattle.

The Great Canadian railroads

There is no greater romance in the development of railways than that of the Canadian Pacific. The whole question of colonizing the vast, uncharted territories of the west was political dynamite in mid-Victorian times, and there were many in England seeking immediate financial reward who deplored the deployment of any effort in Canada when riches seemed more readily to hand elsewhere, in India for example. In Canada itself far-seeing statesmen urged the welding together of the scattered colonies into a single confederation; but while this project was generally accepted in the east, and welcomed as a means of bringing together areas hitherto under the warring British and French influences, on the west coast the isolated colonies of British Columbia and Vancouver Island saw no reason to be associated with Ontario, Quebec and the Maritimes. Yet in eastern Canada it was felt that the very isolation of the colonies on the west coast, shut off by the great and unexplored barrier of the Rocky Mountains, rendered them dangerously susceptible to non-British influences, and liable to absorption by the United States. So an offer was made that if

they would join the Confederation of Canada a railway would be built through the mountains and across the prairies to connect them with the centres of population in the east. The western provinces agreed, and the famous document was duly signed, in Ottawa in July 1870, stating that the railway would be built in ten years.

It was a fantastic commitment. At that time the railways reached no further than 175 miles west of Montreal, and some 2,700 miles of virtually unknown country lay between the 'end of steel' and the Pacific Coast. Romantic though the story of the ensuing years now appears one can be very sure that it never looked that way to those who were involved in it in the fifteen years between the signing of the agreement in 1870 and the driving of the last spike at Craigellachie, British Columbia, in 1885. The political implications and the so-called 'Pacific Scandal' led to the downfall of one government, while the constructional work, whether in high-speed 'mechanized' track-laying across the prairies or in the adventures of the surveyors in trying to find ways through the Rockies and the Selkirks, involved feats of endurance almost without

Below. The British Columbia Railway passes through some of the most beautiful scenery in the west of Canada, and happily some of it, beside Howe Sound, is within easy reach of Vancouver. It is along this line between North Vancouver station and Squamish that seasonal excursion trains are now being run, steam hauled, and using the magnificent *Royal Hudson* 4-6-4 locomotive, formerly of the Canadian Pacific Railway.

Left. A fascinating re-enactment: the Canadian Pacific preserved 4-4-0 with two restored period cars was used during the filming of the television serial *The National Dream*, and is here seen on a branch line in the Rockies where some of the original-type timber trestle viaducts still remain.

Above. Canadian National Railways: the 'U-1-d' class 4-8-2 No. 6043, which ran the last scheduled passenger train to be steam hauled, from The Pas to Winnipeg on April 25, 1960. Now preserved in Assiniboine Park, Winnipeg, Manitoba.

glory on a working engine on the British Columbia Railway, and in the most colourful surroundings imaginable. The main line of the former Pacific Great Eastern, now the British Columbia Railway, runs from North Vancouver, at first beside the mountainous fiord of Howe Sound, to Squamish, and over this section steam-hauled trains are operated with one of the famous *Royal Hudson* type 4-6-4s of the CPR, so named from the part played by one of this class in working the Royal Train during the visit of King George VI and Queen Elizabeth to Canada in 1939. The engines of this class all carried the crown, by Royal permission, but the preserved working engine now carries the name 'British Columbia' over the front buffer beam.

The second great trunk line across Canada, the Canadian National, dates from 1922, after a Government grouping and amalgamation of a number of immensely long single-tracked lines that had been built with more enthusiasm and 'wishful hoping' than sound business acumen, and had become bankrupt, or nearly so, in the process. But they had been vitally needed in World War I, and the Government had taken financial responsibility for them. On amalgamation into the new Canadian National system the route mileage was no less than 22,000! At once a great rationalization and 'streamlining' of services began under the wise and kindly leadership of Sir

parallel. And the picture of that little balloon-stacked 4-4-0 No. 148, standing on the breath-taking trestle viaduct epitomizes the entire story. It was no wonder that that colossus of a general manager, William Cornelius Van Horne, confined his comment to no more than two words when he first rode a locomotive over the western part of the line: 'My God!'

The Canadian Pacific came to possess many splendid steam locomotives in later years, and the passenger types were distinguished by having the cab and tender panels painted in a rich Tuscan red. Appreciation of this led to a change in locomotive colours on the Victorian Railways, in far Australia. Until the early 1900s these latter had been decked in a typical nineteenth-century English colourscheme, of bright green, with brown under frames of a plethora of polished brass and coffee work; but when a new Commissioner arrived from Canada he instituted a change to the Tuscan red of the Canadian Pacific. Apart from museum pieces in Ottawa and elsewhere, the famous livery of the CPR can be seen in all its

Henry Thornton—a man who carried out his reorganization with such tact and consideration for the entire staff that he soon became one of the best-loved of all railway managers. His programme was accompanied by the introduction of enormous new steam locomotives, of which a number are fortunately preserved. Most of these are static open-air museum pieces, enthroned on pedestals at the lineside or in public parks; and examples may be seen at Winnipeg, Capreol, Sarnia and Jasper. The huge 4-8-2 locomotive in the Assininboine Park at Winnipeg was the very last steam locomotive to work a regularly scheduled passenger train, on the remote line running near to the western shores of Hudson Bay between Winnipeg and The Pas.

While it is good to be able to view these engines and study their splendid physical and engineering proportions, nevertheless it is still better to see them in full action, and for operating special excursion trains Canadian National maintains in first-class working order one of these eight-coupled giants. When I was in Canada in 1971 one of the largest ever of the 4-8-4 type, No. 6218, had recently completed her service life. After being superseded by diesels in ordinary traffic, this engine had been retained for special trains; but there are many factors that preclude the indefinite extension of the life of a steam locomotive, and in 1971 the time had come to say 'no more' for the old faithful 6218. Nevertheless so much interest, enthusiasm and a modest increase in revenue had accrued from the running of steam hauled special trains that Canadian National made a survey of the preserved static locomotives to find out which, if any, could most readily be put back into working order to replace 6218. The choice fell on a 4-8-2, No. 6060, which had hitherto been on show at Jasper, in the Rockies. Though not quite such a powerful engine as No. 6218, she had the advantage of being one of a class that had some colour in its painting style. The running plate valences and the tender panels are in a pleasing leaf green; and now, No. 6060, magnificently restored, is running steam hauled specials on Canadian National.

Today all main line traffic in Canada, passenger and freight alike, is worked by diesel-electric locomotives, and these are of two broad types. The first are of the familiar 'first generation' 'nose-cab' design, that became so familiar in a great variety of colourschemes in the USA after World War II. In Canada both the 'Big Two' have changed their locomotive liveries in fairly recent years. The Canadian Pacific naturally included its Tuscan red in the colourscheme on its first diesels, but when under a major re-grouping of the business activities of the great organization the Canadian Pacific Railway became 'CP Rail' a change in colour symbolical of the new

image was made, and the locomotives are now red and white. These same general types can be seen also in the distinctive colours of the Ontario Northland, and the black and white of Canadian National.

Far more numerous, now, than the 'first generation' type, are the less-aesthetically styled but supremely utilitarian 'road freight' type, with their walkways along the outsides. These have been adopted by all the Canadian railways, including mainly mineral lines like the Quebec, North Shore and Labrador, the British Columbia, and the Algoma Central—all with highly distinctive colourschemes – as well as by the 'Big Two'. On heavy express passenger trains one often sees a *possé* of four diesels, two of the 'nose cab' type leading and two 'road freights' coupled to them. In such service speeds up to 90 mph are often called for.

Above left. Canadian National Railways: an historic double-headed combination on an eastbound freight passing through Toronto in April 1952. The leading engine is a 2-10-2 of Class T-I-C, built in 1920 for the Canadian Government Railway. The second engine is a modern 4-8-4.
Left. Canadian Pacific Railway: a Pacific No. 2471, splendidly adorned with the Tuscan red panels, leaving Windsor Station, Montreal, with a commuter train in April 1952.
Top. The Dübs 4-4-0, of 1882, now working on the Prairie Dog Central line, being prepared for the day's work in her berth beside the Canadian National station in Winnipeg. Built in Glasgow for the Canadian Pacific she was sold to the City of Winnipeg Hydro Department in 1918 for use on their private line between Pointe du Bois and Slave Falls. She was retired in 1962 and put into store until taken over by the Prairie Dog Central.
Above. Canadian National: eastbound express for Montreal leaving Toronto, hauled by semi-streamlined 4-8-4 locomotive No. 6402, built 1936 by the Montreal Locomotive Works.

South African locomotives

Down at the Cape, almost in the shadow of Table Mountain, there is a big locomotive depot, Paarden Eiland, where many steam, diesel and electric locomotives are serviced. Cape Town was the birthplace of railways in Southern Africa and from that once remote British colony the prospect of a great trunk line to the north was evolved – not at the outset, it is true, because there was at first little reason to extend communications from the Cape of Good Hope over the barren mountain ranges to the north and across the great inhospitable Karoo desert. It was the discovery of diamonds at Kimberley and then gold in the Transvaal that transformed the whole situation and gave to the Cape Government Railways and its sister enterprise in Natal a strong commercial as well as a colonizing objective, and both extended their tracks towards the mineral riches of the interior. Both railways also assumed a strong strategic significance when war broke out at the end of the nineteenth century.

At first there was no call for speed. The railways were built where nothing save the primitive tracks of the trek wagons had previously existed. After some preliminary building on the 4 ft 8 in gauge the sub-standard gauge of 3 ft 6 in was chosen to save expense and the rails followed the contours of the ground, often on a meandering alignment. But once the great drive to the north was under way, Cecil Rhodes, then Prime Minister of the Cape of Good Hope, proclaimed his great vision of Imperial development, with a 'Cape to Cairo' railway, with his personal slogan: 'The railway is my right hand, and the telegraph is my voice.' Nowhere previously had railways been built in such conditions of torrid heat, waterless countryside and a primitive and often hostile native population. The pioneers who took railroads across the American continent had to fight off the attacks of Indians, but in South Africa the tribes often fought among themselves with the utmost ferocity. It was difficult to get a railway built when reliance had to be placed upon the native population for much of the

Top. One of the condensing '25' class 4-8-4s leaving Oranjerivier, with a heavy freight from De Aar to Kimberley. This is South Africa's busiest steam main line with about 30 trains in each direction daily.
Above. Two '15F' 4-8-2s of the South African Railways on a heavy freight train in rugged country near Karee.
Above right. Two of the huge 25C condensing 4-8-4 locomotives near Kloofeind on the Kimberley–Bloemfontein line with a heavy freight train in April 1970.
Previous page. One of the huge condensing '25C' class 4-8-4s leaving Nelspoort on a northbound goods.

and placed on a pedestal at the south end of Kimberley station. Seventy years ago and more, there were many more staging points for locomotives on the way south dictated by their limited fuel- and water-carrying capacity; but the modern conception of economical steam operation was to work the longest mileages possible, even if it meant a change of engine crew intermediately, and to do this on the more southerly sections of the South African railways meant the development of certain new techniques in engine design. It was not only a case of working over longer distances. Increased luxury of accommodation meant heavier carriages and longer trains, so that locomotives had to be larger as well as capable of running longer mileages in one continuous assignment.

To meet these requirements the tremendous '25C' class locomotives were introduced. These were not only very large in themselves but they were fitted with special tenders in which the exhaust steam was condensed back into water and used again. In this way the water carried in the tanks enabled the locomotive to run much further without replenishment. Of course the equipment necessary to effect this saving in water was expensive and required so much space that the tenders containing it were larger than the engines, enormous though the engines were; but the economies of operation over the desert sections of the great north-to-south main line were such that this high investment was justified. Economies apart, these engines present a mighty spectacle in the stark, arid countryside, whether hauling seemingly endless freights or prestige passenger trains like the *Orange Express* or the *Blue Train*.

Out in the midst of the High Veldt is one of the most remarkable railway centres in the world, De Aar Junction. It is as though the railway activities of Carlisle or York had been set down in the heart of the African wilderness. One reads of towns that have been created by the railway, with great manufacturing plants set up; but De Aar is not one of these. It is a junction pure and simple, but also, like Carlisle and York in the days of British steam, a major staging point for locomotives. Hardly any train, passenger or freight, passes De Aar without changing engines. The line that comes up from the southeast, originating at Port Elizabeth, is nowadays not the main route from that area to the Transvaal, while the fourth line, although the only route into South-West Africa and its capital city of Windhoek, is again secondary to the main 'Cape to Cairo' line – if I may retain Cecil Rhodes's name for it. The line to Windhoek is perhaps the one more beset by water problems than any other in South Africa, and its train service is now entirely operated by diesel locomotives.

But the centre of the action is in the locomotive sheds. In this, also, De Aar

labour force. The traveller of today, riding one of the luxurious trains of the South African Railways northward from the Cape, needs little imagination to picture what things were like in construction days when De Doorns is left behind and the ascent of the Hex River Pass begins. The line is now electric and the smart red-brown locomotives take their heavy trains steadily up the gradient; but it is no wonder that the South African railways developed their steam locomotives to gigantic proportions – 3 ft 6 in gauge notwithstanding.

It was not only a matter of sheer strength to lift trains up the steep gradients. Once the high inland plateau of the Great Karoo desert was attained there was the question of water, which steam locomotives used in plenty. As if to accentuate as vividly as possible the striking development of locomotives in South Africa, one of the early engines of the Cape Government Railways has been restored to its original condition

stands alone. At most of the large steam depots on the South African railways there is an interesting mixture of the vintage and the huge modern locomotives. Most of the veterans are kept in very smart condition by staff to whom steam seems to be the very breath of life. At each of these depots there are high galleries on to which loaded coal wagons are propelled to discharge supplies into the bunkers from which locomotive tenders are recharged. At Paarden Eiland, Port Elizabeth, and at great depots in the Transvaal, work is found for the veterans in pushing the loaded coal trucks, two or three at a time, up on to the high galleries. At De Aar, however, no veterans were to be seen when I was was there last, and the great main-line engines were doing the pushing. Watching a huge 4-8-2 – '15F' class, or even a '23' – charging up the slope I half wondered if the slender steel lattice-work of the gallery would stand the weight of such a great thundering locomotive!

The line northwards from De Aar over the High Veldt to Kimberley is one of the real racing grounds of the modern South African Railways. The maximum speed permitted with steam is 55 mph, but a prestige train such as the *Orange Express* or the *Trans-Karoo Express* coming through a country station with fifteen or sixteen cars on, hauled by one of the giant '25' class 4-8-4 locomotives, with the sun blazing down from cloudless blue African skies, is a marvellous sight, especially when the plat-

forms are thronged with gaily attired native women waiting for the next stopping train. The freights are all fitted with continuous automatic brakes and can also be run at passenger speed. Some of them are made up to enormous lengths and require *two* of the monster engines. A double-header fighting a heavy gradient is always a stirring spectacle, but two Class '25s' in tandem doing 50 mph across the open veldt with a coal train is a sight and sound to remember!

Away from this great main line that leads north from Cape Town to the cities of the Transvaal one meets that astonishing locomotive phenomenon, the Beyer–Garratt articulated. It was conceived some 60 years ago for railways where the going was tough, and over the years it was developed and enlarged to colossal proportions to work on some of the most colourful and spectacular railways in the world. Two predominating conditions govern most routes where the Beyer–Garratt excels: first, that the track can bear no more than a limited axle load, and, second, that it includes many sharp curves and steep gradients. In some areas only one of the conditions is present; but when I first rode on the footplate of a Garratt both were combined in full measure. This was on the celebrated 'Garden Route', never far from the southern coast of South Africa, between Cape Town and Port Elizabeth.

Eastbound, I travelled through the night. On the main 'Cape to Cairo' line we were

electrically hauled as far as Wellington, and there, for the 'Garden Route', one of the Beyer–Garratts took over. Before turning in for the night I rode on the open platform between two coaches, and for a time watched the engine's powerful headlight illuminating the track ahead, through a beautiful wooded country. There were many curves, and the beam of the headlight swung from side to side. I wondered if we might see some game, but we were out of luck that night. Next morning my authority to ride the engine began when we reached Mossel Bay. The Beyer–Garratt type consists essentially of two separate engines fed from one enormous boiler. Each engine has its own chassis and machinery, and the boiler is carried on a cradle suspended from the fore and aft engine units. The 'drive' is applied to a large number of axles so that the weight on any one does not need to be heavy, and the articulation from there, in effect, is in three separate sections – front engine, boiler cradle, rear engine – enabling the complete locomotive to negotiate quite sharp curves with ease.

On the 'Garden Route' there are many sharp gradients to be surmounted as the line makes its way across the valleys and intervening ridges running down to the sea between Mossel Bay and George. But then the really spectacular part of the journey begins – the ascent of the Montagu Pass. While waiting at George one can look up the mountainside and see, hundreds of feet above, the steam of another train. It is so high up it looks like a toy. At first the line makes a complete U-turn and we begin the climb looking back along the coast the way we have just come, towards Mossel Bay. The higher we mount the more magnificent the view becomes, but our driver and fireman have little chance for sightseeing. The hillside becomes increasingly wild and rugged; there is always the chance of boulders or other obstructions on the track and, as this is a hand-fired engine, the fireman is shovelling continuously for a while. We are marshalled with the cab end of the central cradle leading. There are several tunnels to pass through; the line is single-tracked, and in the confined space the exhaust gases and steam from the chimney can be unpleasant, if not actually dangerous. But the chimney is behind us as we climb and, with the windows in the carriages shut for the tunnels, all is well.

Now, at no more than about 15 mph, we are turning into a truly harsh and barren mountain pass. Little by little the wonderful sea view is cut off and the roar of the exhaust beat is flung back at us from stark, almost vertical rock walls. It is interesting to hear that the front and rear engines, though not mechanically connected in any way, are exhausting in unison. Sometimes if there is a momentary wheel slip in one or other of them the beats go out of step and there is a distinct syncopated effect; but very soon they fall into step once again, to provide a single thunderous beat.

For the lighter and branch line workings the South African Railways have two very interesting and thoroughly modern types of fourteen-wheeled steam locomotives, the '19D' 4-8-2 and the '24' class 2-8-4. There are still many hundreds of miles where the largest main line engines are prohibited on account of their weight, and the '19D' is the final development of a long and success-ful series of 4-8-2 designs dating back to 1910, when the first of them, built in Great Britain, was put to work in the Cape. Follow-ing the formation of the Union of South Africa all the former independent state railways were amalgamated to become the South African Railways, and it was over the tracks of the former Cape Government Railways, with its heavy grades and severe curves in the Hex River Pass, that the first 4-8-2s worked. Development of the design was continuous to 1947, when the '19D' was introduced. The later engines of this class, which I have seen working in many parts of Southern Africa, have enormous tenders of the Vanderbilt type that weigh nearly as much as the engine. The water tank is cylindrical and carries no less than 6,250 gallons.

While the '19D' class was designed for routes on which the maximum permitted axle-load is 14 tons, there are many purely branch lines on which the restriction is still more severe. One of these is the very picturesque coastal route eastward from George, in Cape Province. While the main line to Port Elizabeth turns inland and toils up the tremendous climb of the Montagu Pass, the branch continues rarely out of sight of the sea, and here the 2-8-4 engines of the '24' class are used. They are 'lightweights' in every sense, designed for tracks with a maximum axle-load limit of 11 tons. The '24' class, one hundred strong, were built in Glasgow by the North British Locomotive Company, and represent a highly skilled piece of engine designing. One of the most interesting features, to reduce weight, was the incorporation of a one-piece cast steel frame that included the side frame members, cross-stretchers, smokebox saddle and cylinders all in one single casting. It is a design practice that became common enough in the later years of steam locomotive production in the USA, but the South African '24' class were the first built in Great Britain to be so distinguished. I saw some of them under construction in 1949, and twenty years later saw many of them at work in different parts of Africa. Today, of course, the 'winds of change' are affecting the South African Railways. It is a major point of policy to change over to electric traction where possible. There are ample reserves of coal in the country for generation of electricity, and it is a matter of making the necessary capital available. In the meantime the steam locomotives are not getting any younger. The great firms in Europe from which the South African Railways previously obtained their steam power are no longer building steam, and spare parts are be-coming increasingly difficult to get. So certain sections are being turned over to diesel traction, particularly the lines across desert country, south and west of De Aar Junction. The giant '25C' class 4-8-4s, with condensing tenders, designed specially for the near-waterless sections of the Cape main line south of De Aar, are being transferred to the sections north to Kimberley and Bloemfontein, and are having their condensing gear removed.

It was in Natal that the Beyer–Garratt first won its spurs. When first introduced, designers of orthodox engines looked upon it as something of a freak, a rather im-probable conception. In the USA, as mentioned elsewhere in this book, the Mallet form of articulation was well es-tablished for slow-haul heavy-grade work and on the Natal section of the South African Railways, where there is a very long and severe incline from Durban up to the Cato Ridge, some very large Mallet articul-ated locomotives, built in Scotland, were securely entrenched and held in high favour. There was healthy competition, however, between various British firms in the loco-motive-building business, and Beyer Peacock's of Manchester, who had acquired the manufacturing rights for the Garratt type of locomotive, secured an order for one

Right above. The Port Elizabeth–Cape Town express climbing to the summit of the Montagu Pass. The locomotive is one of the GMA class Beyer-Garratts, which work the train over the very steeply graded section between Oudtshoorn and Mossel Bay. The auxiliary water tank attached to these engines can be seen ahead of the leading coach.
Right below. The *Blue Train*, hauled by two electric locomotives, is the pride of the modern South African railway network. Plying between Cape Town and Johannesburg and Pretoria, it is one of the most luxurious trains in the world, with private suites, observation lounge, and air-conditioning for the 26-hour journey.

experimental unit, for trial in Natal. So, just as Shap and the wild mountain country of the Settle and Carlisle line in England had been and continued to be the scene of momentous locomotive trials, the great climb from Durban into the Drakensberg Mountains witnessed a battle of railway giants in South Africa.

The contest proved a triumph for the Beyer–Garratt type of locomotive and it brought to the fore a young South African engineer, W. Cyril Williams, who was nominated invigilator on these important trials. He wrote a report so heavily in favour of the Garratt as to earn a reproof from his chief mechanical engineer – so firmly was the Mallet type held in high favour. But Williams stuck to his guns, and in a further prolonged series of trials the superiority of the Garratt was clearly proved. Williams thereupon left his employment on the South African Railways and sailed for England, where he walked into the office of *The Railway Gazette* in London. Granted an interview with the Editor, he said simply: 'I've come to sell Garratts.' Eventually he did sell many million pounds' worth, and nowhere more successfully than to his first employees, the South African Railways.

Around Johannesburg, 'The Golden City', the railway tracks are often bordered

Left. Heavy pulling in Cape Province: the Mossel Bay–Johannesburg express on the 1 in 40 gradient to Lootsberg summit hauled by two Class '19D' 4-8-2 locomotives, Nos. 2643 and 2704.
Above. On the Rosemead–Graaf Reinet line Cape Province: one of the powerful branch line '19D' class 4-8-2s on a freight train near Erin, No. 2714.
Pages 98, 99. One of the lightweight branch 2-8-4s of Class '24' on the morning goods train from Knysna to George passes the mouth of the Kaimaans River.

by the conical golden-coloured spoil heaps of the mines. The frequent winds send yellow dust flying over all the equipment; it gets into every crevice and makes the gasketing of vital machinery more necessary here, perhaps, than in torrential rain or the sandstorms of desert lands. But the spoil heaps of the Reef add a distinctive and colourful touch to the lines on which set out express trains to still more distant parts of Africa. Rhodes's 'Cape to Cairo' line skirted the western frontiers of the two Boer republics, and from Kimberley made its way through the Bechuanaland protectorate to Mafeking. After the South African war this became an important junction, where a line westwards from Johannesburg joined the 'Cape to Cairo' route.

steam that the engines are mechanically stoked; no one man could shovel coal at the rate these Beyer–Garratts consume it on such duties.

Rudyard Kipling wrote about 'romance bringing up the nine-fifteen'; but if ever there was a line steeped in romance it was that which Cecil Rhodes saw as eventually running from 'Cape to Cairo', as anyone who has read George Pauling's *Chronicles of a Contractor* will realize. 'Georgie Porgie', as Cecil Rhodes called him, the gigantic, supremely colourful civil engineer who built many hundreds of miles of the 'Cape to Cairo' railway, has left a monument as enduring as the Pyramids, and nowhere more so than in the continuation of the line northwards from Bulawayo to

Above. Pacifics at Bloemfontein: a '16E' class leaves with a pick-up goods to Springfontein, about to cross the flyover, while in the foreground a '16A' waits, on another pick-up duty.
Right. In the Toorwaterpoort: a freight from Oudtshoorn to Klipplaat, in rugged country, is distinguished by an immaculate '19D' 4-8-2.
Pages 102, 103. On the picturesque branch from George to Knysna, Cape Province, which runs by the sea for most of its 42 miles, a mixed train crosses the Kaaimans River bridge hauled by one of the lightweight 2-8-4 locomotives of Class '24', No. 3670.

This cross-country line through the north-western Transvaal was another one that presented steam locomotive operators with water problems. The economic situation here was not such as to justify using the great '25' class 4-8-4s with their condensing tenders, and instead a class of very large Beyer–Garratts was introduced, to which was attached a huge auxiliary water tank. These engines were used on the through express trains between Johannesburg and the cities of Rhodesia. The Beyer–Garratts work on the 128-mile section between Krugersdorp (Johannesburg) and Zeerust, where the ruling gradient is as steep as 1 in 40, and where there are only three places intermediately where a locomotive can get water. At Krugersdorp the line is nearly 6,000 ft above sea level, and it descends at one point to little more than 3,500 ft. This is indeed railroading in the raw, where sharp curves, steep gradients, and desert conditions are all combined. The working here makes such demands for the crossing of the Zambesi river at the Victoria Falls. Only once, and then no more than briefly, does the scenery become spectacular; but there is history and atmosphere in almost every station name, and the farther one drives north from Bulawayo the greater are the chances of meeting nature in the raw. The 'stations' are mostly no more than passing places where two long trains can pass each other, and the appearance of the countryside is epitomized by the station name Igusi – more correctly Gusu, in Sindebele – which describes the sandy, scrub-covered land thereabouts.

From Sawmills, the next important station, lying in a pleasant valley, the line climbs once again to the low bush country and runs dead straight for miles, and it is here that one can meet wild life in earnest. Not infrequently elephants stray on to the line, and are sometimes hit, with gory consequences, by the big Garratt locomotives. I was coming up from the Victoria Falls one moonlight night on an engine of the Mail, and we saw a large herd of elephants making their way through thick bush; and immediately afterwards, as we were approaching a little station, round a curve, the driver clutched my arm and said, 'Look.' There, drinking at the foot of the water column, was a lioness. She made off as soon as our headlight picked her up; but not long ago there was a real wild-life disaster on this same line, when a freight train going at full speed ran into a whole pride of lions, and killed four of them

outright. Riding on the Garratts can be an exciting business on the 'Cape to Cairo' line!

The great spectacle is of course the viaduct over the gorge of the Zambesi river beside the Victoria Falls. The midpoint of this magnificent bridge is now an international frontier. Cecil Rhodes himself never saw the Falls, but the stupendous sight they present, together with the curtain of spray that is always rising, appealed so much to his imagination that he decreed the 'Cape-to-Cairo' line should not only cross the gorge at a point where passengers could see the Falls in all their glory, but near enough for the carriages to be bathed in the spray. Today, unfortunately, no passenger trains cross the bridge and visitors clad in water-proofs walk to the rain forest to be drenched by the spray.

Above. In the mountains near Fourth Reverse: a '19D' class 4-8-2 is working a freight on the Barkly East branch.
Right. Near the end of the long branch from Aliwal North to Barkly East a '19D' class 4-8-2 crosses a picturesque river viaduct.

Steam in Australia

Steam traction has practically disappeared from the various state railways of Australia, and entirely so from New Zealand, so far as regular services are concerned. The history of the railways could be called chequered, owing in part to the diversity of rail gauges. For example, New South Wales adopted the British 4 ft 8½ in, while Victoria and South Australia decided upon the Irish 5 ft 3 in, with inevitable confrontation and age-long inconvenience of interchange at the state boundaries. Then there was the pioneering of long, single-tracked lines into the seemingly limitless 'outback'. How these railways are now being gradually connected up is one of the greatest romances of modern transport, even though the traction is diesel, except on the commuter lines of Sydney and Melbourne.

In all the states there are railway museums, some at present only in the assembly stage; but in the vicinity of Adelaide, Brisbane and Melbourne there are magnificent collections of historic locomotives. The dry Australian climate is a great

advantage here, because these large and impressive assemblies are out of doors. In addition to these static exhibits a number of historic locomotives have been preserved in full operating condition and are used frequently for special trips sponsored by the Association of Railway Enthusiasts or the Australian Historical Railway Society. For the most part these trips have the enthusiastic backing of the railway administrations in the various states. Some of them involve long mileages and a wealth of careful organization beforehand.

Originally the locomotive colour in most of the states was black. That of New South Wales was inspired by the style of the London and North Western Railway, and exemplified today on the splendid little 2-4-0 *Hardwicke*, preserved in the National Railway Museum of Great Britain, at York. There had been a green livery prior to 1890 in New South Wales, of which a superb example can be seen on the old outside-cylindered 4-4-0 preserved on a pedestal at Canberra. But for 'Old English' splendour in locomotive liveries that of the Victorian

Railways up to the turn of the century had few equals, even at home in Great Britain. The Victorian steam locomotives preserved in the open-air museum at North Williamstown, near Melbourne, have a rather watered-down version, retaining the bright green, it is true, but with plain black and white lining instead of a gorgeous array of red, yellow and brown, with much ornamental brass and copper work.

It was curious that while Victoria turned to plain, unadorned black in the last years of steam traction, Queensland, South Australia, and Western Australia went gay with bright new colours. The tank engines working the Brisbane suburban services, for example, were painted sky-blue, and in

Left. New South Wales: the 'AD60' class Beyer-Garratts were the most powerful locomotives on the standard gauge in Australia. Of the number supplied, only one remained in working order in 1975, here seen broadside-on working a special train.
Top. New South Wales: the preserved 'C32' class 4-6-0 No. 3203 with a special train in 1975 on the Sydney to Melbourne main line near Menangle Park.
Above. New South Wales: one of the very famous 'C32' class 4-6-0s, originally 'P6' and dating from 1890, at Clyde, near Sydney, on a special trip in 1975.

Western Australia the fine new main-line engines introduced in the 1950s were painted in a handsome shade of leaf green. Examples of all these colourschemes have fortunately been preserved, including one of the big Queensland Beyer–Garratts in 'Derby red'. When from 1925 onwards South Australia suddenly decided to double the haulage capacity of its main-line locomotives, the enormous new engines built in England began life in plain black; but in their later years they were 'dolled up' to some extent, with the running-plate valences painted green and the smokebox fronts painted aluminium silver. The enginemen nicknamed them 'Palefaces'!

The New South Wales Government railways had a distinguished history of locomotive development, from the Scottish inspired 'P6' class 4-6-0 of 1891 to the massive 'C38' Pacifics of 1943. These latter engines were still in main-line service when I first went to Australia in 1969, and I rode one of them on the *Newcastle Flyer* service from Gosford northwards. Apart from enjoying a hard steam ride, with speeds up to 70 mph, I was very interested to find that the enginemen worked through from Sydney to Newcastle, although half the mileage is electrified. They took the electric locomotive from Sydney, and then at the halfway point would be prepared to work either steam or diesel for the rest of the journey. So far as I know this was the only instance anywhere in the world of enginemen not only 'swopping horses', but swopping the form of motive power as well. The route includes the crossing of the supremely beautiful Hawkesbury River, with its numerous creeks and only the oyster beds to dispel any momentary thoughts an Englishman from the West Country might have that he was back in Cornwall.

The Victorian Railways, like those of Great Britain, were worked almost to death in World War II, and afterwards recovery was made under a plan known as 'Operation Phoenix'. It included the purchase of many new steam locomotives, among which were the very powerful 'R' class 4-6-4s for heavy express passenger work. A concession towards colour was made on these engines. While unlined black was still the basis, the running-plate valences and the small smoke-reflecting plates on each side of the smokebox were painted a vivid pillar-box red. An order for 70 of these engines was placed with the North British Locomotive Company of Glasgow; but they never really fulfilled the task for which they were ordered. The change to diesel traction began very soon after their first introduction, and to get full money's worth out of the expensive new power the diesels had to be allocated to the longest and hardest duties.

Until comparatively recently Victoria and South Australia were the only two states with a common boundary to have the same rail gauge, and for a long time the *Interstate Express* was the only train by which one could travel from one state capital to another without having to change between Melbourne and Adelaide. The train of today, enormously heavier but not much faster, is the *Overland*; but although it is well patronized very few of its passengers could tell you much about the intervening country because the journey is done through the night. The frontier station of Serviceton, where the locomotives and crews of the Victorian railways hand over to those of South Australia, is itself something of an enigma. In earlier days the only people likely to get out would be smugglers arrested when interstate customs were imposed; and the station was provided with dungeons for the safekeeping of these miscreants.

In the last stages of the long run from

Left. New South Wales: a 2-8-2 tank engine on the Richmond Vale Railway, an industrial serving the coal industry. At the time the photograph was taken, in August 1975, the locomotive, No. 10 *Richmond Main* was 64 years old, and still in original condition.
Below. New South Wales Government Railways: the first five of this class of thirty 'Pacifics', dating from 1943, were partially streamlined and painted green. The rest were black. Engine No. 3801, pictured here in South Australia in 1972, is preserved in working order for special trains.

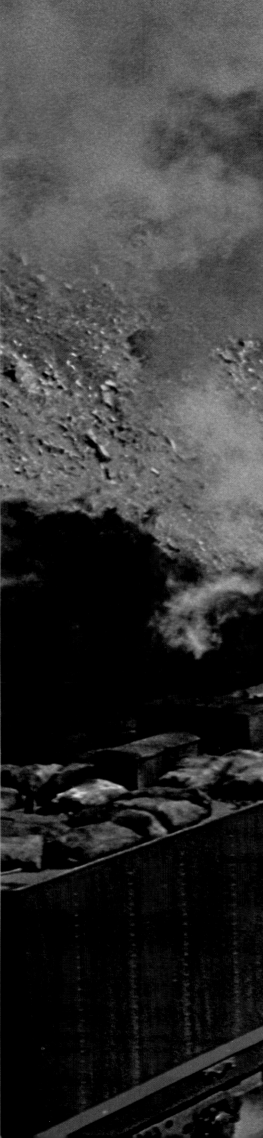

Serviceton to Adelaide South Australian locomotives had to work their hardest in climbing the severe gradients of the Mount Lofty Range, with the incessant curvature. It was for taking trains like the *Overland* that the 'Palefaces' were built. There were, nevertheless, other parts of the South Australian railways where such heavy locomotives could not be used and were in fact not needed by the ruling gradients, and a very elegant 4-8-4 design was brought in during World War II, semi-streamlined and incorporating some of the most advanced techniques of the day. The form of streamlining on these engines had its inspiration from some gigantic express locomotives of the Pennsylvania Railroad; and for the first time in South Australia they were all named. The first to be put into traffic was named after the Governor, Sir Malcolm Barclay-Harvey, himself a railway enthusiast and author of a fine book about a colourful little railway in his home country, the north of Scotland, running from Aberdeen up to Elgin and also working the Royal Deeside line to Ballater. This engine is now preserved in full working order.

The railways of South Australia began with the 5ft 3in gauge, linking up with those of Victoria at Serviceton, but events elsewhere led to the introduction, within the one state, of a second gauge. When railways began in Queensland and Western Australia the territories were so far removed from other railway activities that little chance was foreseen of their eventually linking up, and as cost was a major consideration in those developing lands the decision was taken in both states to adopt the 3ft 6in gauge. In South Australia there were remote tracts where railways were needed, but not to the extent of having the spacious 5ft 3in of the interstate main line; and so these feeder lines were also built on the 3ft 6in gauge. In the museum just outside Adelaide preserved examples of the small 3ft 6in gauge locomotives can be studied alongside an enormous 'Paleface' and its heavy freight

Right. Victorian Railways: one of the powerful 'R' class 4-6-4s — part of 'Operation Phoenix' — on an A.H.R.S. special to Ballarat in 1971.
Above. Victorian Railways: a spectacular view of a 'K' class lightweight 2-8-0, No. 184, en route for Ballarat in 1971.

Left. South Australian Railways: the preserved 4-8-4 *Sir Malcolm Barclay-Harvey* on a special from Adelaide to Truro in August 1975.
Below. South Australian Railways: the first of the lightweight 4-8-4s *Sir Malcolm Barclay-Harvey*, as newly restored in 1972, and working a special train. The form of streamlining on these engines was derived from the contemporary 4-4-4-4 express passenger class of the Pennsylvania Railroad.

equivalent. But there is also a 4-6-0 of the 4 ft 8½ in gauge. Three gauges in the one state?—and that 4-6-0 looks suspiciously like a standard New South Wales design. How did this come about?

At the end of the nineteenth century the British Government in London was anxious to bring the hitherto independent colonies into a unified federation, in the same way as had been so successfully achieved in Canada. At first Western Australia stood out against the project. She was isolated from the rest not only by great distance, but also by the vast extent of the intervening desert land, where there were no trees, no vegetation, no animals, no people — absolutely nothing. Recalling the curiously similar situation of some 30 years earlier in Canada, where British Columbia, separated from the rest by the great barrier of the Rocky Mountains, had resisted the idea of being included in the Confederation, the Imperial Government made exactly the same proposal to Western Australia as they

Above. Two out of the three gauges at Port
Pirie: at left a South Australian 5ft 3in gauge
'Pacific' No. 621, and at right a New South
Wales standard gauge 4-6-0 No. 3642, Engine
No. 621, now named *Duke of Edinburgh*, is
preserved in full operating condition.
Right. One of the maroon-painted 'C17' class
4-8-0s of the Queensland Railways on a rail-
tour up the Monkland-Brooloo branch in April
1975.
Previous pages. On the 3ft 6in gauge in South
Australia. A pair of 'T' class 2-8-0s, Nos. 186
and 199, of 1903 vintage on an A.H.R.S.
special from Peterborough to Quorn in 1970.

had done to British Columbia: if Western
Australia would join, a railway would be
built to connect it up with the others.
Western Australia agreed, and the Commonwealth came into being in 1901. The
promise of a railway meant constructing a
line across the utter 'nothingness' of the
Nullarbor Plain. The word 'nullarbor' means
no trees – but there was nothing else either,
particularly water. The line was to be built
under Commonwealth auspices, and there
arose at once the question of the gauge. At
Kalgoorlie, the western end, there was the
3ft 6in gauge of Western Australia; at the
eastern end the 5ft 3in of South Australia.
By chance, wise beyond anything that was
foreseen at the time, the Commonwealth
railways decided on the British and New
South Wales standard of 4ft 8½in. And so,
for a period that lasted for more than 50
years, there was a 'break of gauge' at both
ends, and trains on three gauges running
into the South Australian station of Port
Pirie.

It is an amazing journey from Port Pirie
westwards across the Nullarbor Plain. In
1969 when I enjoyed this trip we came up
from Adelaide in a 5ft 3in gauge train, and
there, late in the afternoon, transferred to
the 'Trans', as railwaymen then called it.
This was to be our 'home', our travelling
hotel, for nearly two days. After the sun had
set in a cloudless sky and we drove on into
a darkness punctuated only by the flashing

brilliance of the stars, I felt that we were
indeed going out into the blue. Soon after
sunrise next morning, when we stopped at
Cook for servicing and change of engine
crew, I went forward to ride in the cab of
the leading diesel. I looked ahead down a
single line of rails, disappearing in a
perfectly straight line into the far distance
across a limitless expanse of dwarf scrub-
land. Believe it or not, the line is absolutely
straight for 297 miles across this incredible
'nothingness', with the soft bluish-grey of
the scrub mixed with the dun colour of the
sand under the dazzling brilliance of the
cloudless sky. Soon we were running at
55–60 mph, and kept this up steadily for
mile after mile. As we approached the next
station objects began to appear like the first
sight of ships at sea – the tops first, literally
over the curve of the earth's surface. When
we travelled, the new standard-gauge line
had been built from Kalgoorlie to Perth and
we did not have to change on reaching
Western Australian metals. Since that time
the standard-gauge link east of Port Pirie
has been completed and the magnificent
Indian-Pacific express runs through from
Perth to Sydney entirely on this 4ft 8½in
gauge.

If one wishes to recapture something of
the pioneering spirit of Australian railways
one must ride 'The Ghan' to Alice Springs.
It runs over a line north from Port Augusta
that was part of a companion to the Nullarbor

route, providing a continuous south-to-north link and eventually reaching Port Darwin. But although construction started from both ends the link-up was never made and the line from the south got no further than Alice Springs. Before the railway came, transport was entirely by camel and the name of the only passenger train is derived from the Afghans, who led the camel caravans over this desert country. Even now that diesel locomotives have replaced steam locomotives, and 'The Ghan' has dining cars throughout its long journey, the trip is not to be lightly undertaken. To travel from Port Augusta to Alice Springs and back takes five days.

In steam days, on 3ft 6in gauge, 'The Ghan' was hauled by locomotives of Queensland design, distinguished among all other Australian locomotives by the ornamental sandbox on the boiler top, between the chimney and the dome. In Queensland itself locomotives of this type are now little more than treasured museum pieces, though at one time they were used on specials over the highly scenic line from Cairns, at the terminus of the long main line up from Brisbane, to Kuranda and the Atherton Plains. Climbing the gradient from Cairns the line passes on a slender trestle almost within the spray of a spectacular waterfall. Kuranda station is one of outstanding beauty. It is not far removed from a halt among a profusion of tropical ferns. There

cannot be many railway stations that are a popular tourist sight; but Kuranda is certainly one of them.

One would not ordinarily expect to find interesting locomotives on iron-ore railway lines, but there are two major instances of this in Western Australia. It was the need for mass transport of ore from the great deposits at Koolyanobbing to the refinery at Kwinana, beside Fremantle on the Indian Ocean, that justified the building of the standard-gauge line from Kalgoorlie to the west coast. Today the railway acts like some gigantic conveyor belt, 310 miles long, from the mines to the refinery, and over it thunder at 50 mph trains of 96 cars, hauled by three 3,300 horsepower diesel locomotives, with a trailing load of nearly 10,000 tons. To stand at the lineside in the beautiful Avon valley and see one of these trains roar past – half-a-mile long, and headed by the three blue and white locomotives – makes one realize that steam does not hold the monopoly on excitement and colour.

If the diesel-operated ore trains on the State railway are colourful, what can I say of the Hamersley Iron Railway, up in the north west? The standard-gauge line west of Kalgoorlie is a general purpose railway, carrying the transcontinental *Indian–Pacific* express, fast local railcar services, grain in large block loads in addition to iron ore; but Hamersley, again connecting huge

The *Indian-Pacific*, drawn by a WAGR diesel unit, heads eastwards near the start of its 2461-mile haul from Perth to Sydney. The service was inaugurated in 1970 and now comprises four air-conditioned trains a week in each direction. The journey takes three days at an average speed of 38 mph.

mineral deposits with the port of shipment at Dampier, was built as a single-purpose 'conveyor belt', set in the stark, barren, but intensely colourful land of the north-west. For the entire landscape is the red colour of iron ore, and this amazing railway, 182 miles of first-class heavy main-line track, was built to carry a payload of 15,000 tons per train. When the line was first opened, to the new mining centre of Tom Price, these trains represented a gross trailing load of 18,000 tons, in 152 cars. But with the opening of the extension to Parraburdoo some trains are made up of no less than 186 cars. Because the gradients are generally in favour of loaded trains no more than three locomotives are required for this tremendous load of 22,000 tons. The locomotives sport a vivid colourscheme of bright blue and yellow, in startling contrast to the prevailing red of the countryside and the dazzling white of the salt pans near Dampier. On the extension line from Tom Price to Parraburdoo, which was completed only in 1972, the newly excavated cuttings, some of them very deep, showed up the many brilliant colours of the varying strata of naked rock, providing an amazing background to the passage of these heavy trains.

Before the building of the standard gauge line westwards from Kalgoorlie, the Western Australian Government Railways were an exclusively 3ft 6in gauge system and some extensive modernization of steam

motive power took place after World War II. The operating conditions are severe, not so much in their demands for high or long-sustained outputs of power, as in the terrain and in the characteristics of the coal available in large quantities in the south-west of the State. A high proportion of the total railway mileage permitted no greater axle loads than 10 tons and yet powerful new locomotives were needed. The indigenous coal burns slowly, with a long flame, and fireboxes of specialized proportions were needed to burn this to the best advantage. Another basic requirement was to minimize the emission of sparks. In the hot summers, the whole countryside is highly susceptible to bush fires and every precaution had to be taken to lessen the chances of these being started by locomotives. So that while providing every incentive to rapid combustion of a somewhat reluctantly burning coal, this could not be done by the easy expedient of a sharp blast, and instead spark arrestors had to be fitted.

All these requirements were successfully incorporated into the new 4-8-2s introduced in 1951. They were built in England by Beyer, Peacock and Company, a firm which had a distinguished record of vast mechanical engineering exports in the Beyer-Garratt articulated locomotives. In the Western Australian 'W' class 4-8-2s their designing experience and ingenuity was taxed considerably. Externally, the new

engines were distinguished by a handsome new livery of pale green, whereas previous steam locomotives in the State had been red-brown. Inside a notably neat and compact outline was packed a wealth of locomotive 'know-how' that resulted in a remarkably successful traffic unit. The 'W' class was followed by a much larger version, having the 2-8-2 wheel arrangement, for working over those sections of line where larger locomotives were permitted. Although designated for freight duties, these also had the smart colourscheme in light green.

Finally, a word on preserved steam in New Zealand. The two locomotives used for the 'tourist' run in the south of South Island have a long history of hard and noble work on the main lines of New Zealand, and this makes the 'Kingston Flyer' the object of much affection by all railway lovers. The New Zealand railways have been served by many notable locomotive designs, but none better for their size and weight than the 'Ab' 'Pacifics', introduced in 1915 and eventually multiplied to a stud of 152. Today these two working survivors, kept in exhibition condition with everything that can be polished simply glittering, take turns to roll their train placidly over the 38 miles from Lumsden to Kingston in 80 minutes; and the class as a whole will be remembered for the 30-odd years when they were the mainstay of the New Zealand railways motive power stud.

Above left. One of the most characteristic sights in north Queensland is the immense fields of sugar cane, and 2ft gauge railways are used to bring the crops to the main line stations. Here, a little 0-6-0 named *Melbourne* brings a load from Trebonne, near Ingham.

Top. 'The Ghan' en route to Alice Springs, in the days when that train was steam hauled. The locomotive is one of the Queensland-type 4-8-0s, working on the 3ft 6in gauge.
Above. Queensland Railways: one of the 'B18¼' class 'Pacifics' at Caboolture, on a special to Gympie, on the Brisbane–North Queensland main line.

Steam in Japan

In the period of recovery after the terrible earthquake of 1923, which caused such catastrophic damage in Tokyo and Yokohama and inevitably much serious disruption and destruction on the railways, much important modernization work was started. Even before the earthquake disaster, however, the Japanese railways had advanced a long way beyond their early habits, which in casual ways and a total inability to hurry made them something of a curiosity to visitors from countries which, by the end of the nineteenth century, had trains regularly topping 80 mph in their daily running and intense commuter services. The technical foundations were sound enough, with two famous English engineers, W M Smith, and R F Trevithick, successively acting as Locomotive Super-intendent. The second of these two was a grandson of the great Cornish pioneer of steam traction, Richard Trevithick, and was the first man to build a locomotive in Japan.

In other respects, however, there were hampering legacies from the early days, such as roundabout, sharply curving routes, built thus to minimize constructional costs but a hindrance when the management in the first years of the twentieth century wanted to put on faster trains. There was also the rail gauge, which had originally been fixed at 3ft 6in to lessen costs; and the structural clearance limits did not eventually permit of huge locomotives like those now running in South Africa, also on the 3ft 6in. Tunnels were frequent, and fine civil engineering work in bridges and station layouts was amply evident.

At the same time the Japanese railways, more perhaps than any others in the world, had a constant task in taking every possible precaution against earthquake damage. Of course the terrible occurrence of 1923 was altogether exceptional; but since the back-bone of the main island of Honshu is a chain of not-so-extinct volcanoes, anything can happen. The risk of earthquake damage is something that the Japanese railways have just got to live with. There is in constant readiness an organization for rapid attention to 'incidents', in the same way as precautions against air-raid damage were highly organized in all the belligerent countries in World War II.

British influence was strong in the early days and it is not surprising that many of the earlier locomotives were built by English and Scottish firms. However, they did include certain distinctive features specified first by W M Smith and then by Trevithick. Around the year 1910 Japanese locomotives had begun to have a definite 'family look', and this is to be seen in the several interesting types of the pre-1914 period preserved in the fascinating 'live steam' museum at Kyoto. Examples of two vintage classes were still in revenue-earning service in Japan in 1973. One of these was the massive '9600' class 2-8-0 freight engine, the first introduction of which dates back to 1913. Japanese locomotives of that period had a neatness of outline that revealed their British genealogy, though already in order to give easier accessibility many of the accessories were being mounted along the running plates. Another long-lived class of their period is the '8620' 2-6-0 of 1914 – a fast mixed-traffic type – which by its very length of service of nearly 60 years displays its excellence of design and general usefulness.

Today, in the main island of Honshu, one finds the most extreme contrasts in railways that it is possible to imagine. The original 3ft 6in gauge main line from Tokyo to Shimonoseki, generally following the coast, is electrified throughout and has been much upgraded to permit faster running, carrying all the freight traffic and long-distance passenger trains to the remoter parts of the country that involve overnight journeys and sleeping cars. The electric locomotives are painted in gay colours and immaculately maintained; but such a railway, however efficiently run, could not hope

Left. One of the veteran '9600' class 2-8-0s No. 69665, on a freight train on the Hohi line, in Kyushu, and passing a display of blossom on the cutting side.
Above. A pair of veteran '8620' class 2-6-0s toiling uphill on the Hanawa Line, in Northern Honshu, in a snow covered landscape.

123

Above. Two of the standard 'C58' class 2-6-2 engines seen broadside on, in wintry weather on the Rikuto Line, in northern Honshu.
Left. The *Niseko Express*, from Hakodate to Sapporo, in the northern island of Hokkaido, double-headed, with a 'D51' general purpose 2-8-2 leading a 4-6-4 of Class 'C62'.

to meet the needs of a country now so highly industrialized along its east coast, and which had thrown off its traditional leisurely habits to become a nation of the greatest hustlers in the world – and incredible travellers. Even before World War II plans were in gestation for an entirely new and much straighter main line between Tokyo and Osaka, but it was not until 1964 that the new Shinkansen line, roughly paralleling the ancient Tokaido trail, was brought into service.

'New' indeed! Nothing like it had ever been seen previously on the railways of the world. An entirely new route was engineered, on the 4ft 8½in gauge, cutting straight through every obstruction, mountains and valleys alike, and so straight that a speed of 130 mph could be maintained without a break from end to end. There is a breathtaking splendour in its engineering and in the magnificent electrical technology that enables the entire railway, 320 miles of it, to be regulated from a single control room near Tokyo, and the exact position of every train seen at any minute. There are quite a few trains too. Every fifteen minutes from 6 am one of these Hikari, or lightning trains, leaves Tokyo for Osaka, each one with a cruising speed of 130 mph, and the procession continues without a break until 9 pm – each one carrying, on an average, a *thousand* passengers. And a similar procession is winging its way northwards to Tokyo.

The central mountain chain that forms an almost continuous backbone from north to south in the island of Honshu provides a stiff obstacle to those sections of the railways that have to provide cross-country communication with the west coast, and there are many picturesque locations where steam locomotives can still be seen fighting severe gradients against a rugged mountain background. When modernization of the steam locomotive stock began in the 1930s, a range of new designs was worked out, all having a 'family likeness', but an entirely new look. While reflecting much technical excellence, that 'new look' was at once gaunt, angular and starkly functional. The new classes came eventually to include large batches of the 2-6-2, 4-6-2, 2-8-2, and 4-6-4 types, not only very sound in their basic design, but manufactured with precision and remarkably smooth and quiet in their operation.

The 'C58' class of 2-6-2 is essentially for light branch lines, and they could be seen working in the mountain passes in North Honshu. One of the most noticeable characteristics of the standard steam locomotive is the grouping together under a single elongated casing of all the mountings on the top of the boiler, thus to include the sandbox and steam dome, leaving only the chimney, safety valves and the electric generator as separate projections. The generator is mounted just ahead of the cab and is an important accessory, because operating regulations require that all trains should run with headlights on even in the brightest sunshine. Another external feature is the 'boxpok' type of cast-steel driving-wheel centres – quite unlike the usual form of spoked locomotive wheel.

To see Japanese steam operating in its most colourful and spectacular form one had to travel to the northern island of Hokkaido, for it was there that the largest of all passenger locomotives of the JNR saw their last regular service on the express trains between Hakodate, the ferry terminal, and Sapporo, the capital city. The 'C62' class, of the 4-6-4 type, are very large and impressive engines. I have seen one of them in steam at the museum roundhouse in Kyoto, but enthusiasts from all over Japan used to travel north to see and photograph them as they thundered over the mountain route between Oshiamambe and Otaru – often two of them to a train, and on some heavy duties one sometimes saw triple heading. It was said that the waiting room of Kamimcha station, on the line, was always crowded with railway enthusiasts anxious to photograph a pair of 'C62' engines in action.

This section of line provided exceedingly colourful action for those who ventured north in the winter months. The climate in Hokkaido is severe, with heavy snowfalls. When I was there in April 1973 the mountain tops were still covered, and in the deep gullies on the hill sections of the railway there were many places where the deep drifts had not entirely melted away. Locomotives working in these conditions were equipped with two headlights, usually one on each of the smoke-deflecting plates so as to get the best possible lookout ahead during snowstorms. The express service between Hakodate and Sapporo is now operated by multiple-unit diesel trains, very smartly coloured, but without the emotional appeal of a noisy, black, smoke-belching steam locomotive.

The term 'smoke-belching' is no idle phrase where steam-locomotive operation in Hokkaido is concerned; for the Munhoran main line, following the sea coast and then turning inland through the important junction of Numanohatta, is an important coal-train route operated by one of the most numerous of the Japanese standard steam-locomotive classes, the 'D51' 2-8-2, of which more than 1,100 were built. I should explain that the prefix letters in Japanese locomotive numerology denote the number of coupled axles. 'C' has three coupled axles, whether the actual type is, for example, a 2-6-2 (C58), a 4-6-2 (C57) or a 4-6-4 (C62). The 'D51' has four coupled axles, and was first introduced in 1938. Engines of this class were to be seen in most parts of Japan where steam-operated freight trains ran.

In Hokkaido they were doing a great deal of very hard work. Watching them from

the lineside there were certainly some interesting features to be noted. For example, there was the extraordinary quietness of their running. With locomotives engaged in heavy freight service one is accustomed to a certain amount of noise and clanking, particularly when drifting with the regulator closed; but these 'D51s' were going about their jobs like so many sewing machines. The Japanese railwaymen who accompanied me were constantly warning me not to be caught unawares when one of them was approaching, in almost complete silence. But what they lacked in noise they made up for in full measure in the sight of their exhausts. I have never – repeat never! – seen so much black smoke thrown out; and while this can often be the delight of the photographer, if the wind happens to be blowing the wrong way one can secure nothing more than a headlight and a vast black cloud.

In the southernmost island of Kyushu, as in Hokkaido, the intense industrialism of the east coast of Honshu is left far behind, and in the beautiful country south of Beppu the railway runs through a succession of enticing coastal scenes, rich farmland, and the limitless expanse, in many places, of the rice fields. The use of steam was diminishing when I was in Kyushu, but in the far south, at Miyazaki, there was a photographer's

paradise. The station and yard are interesting and there are excellent viewpoints from which trains crossing the long viaduct over the estuary of the River Oyodo can be photographed, but it was at Miyazaki also that I saw the Japanese Royal Train. It had not long previously arrived and the engine was still carrying its decorations. They consisted of two national flags arranged crosswise on the front of the smokebox and the traditional gilded chrysanthemum just above the centre of the buffer beam. The engine itself, a 'C57' class Pacific, was of course superbly cleaned up, with many additional embellishments and everything that could be polished not merely polished but *burnished*.

The railway system on the island of Kyushu is connected with that on the mainland of Honshu by a tunnel under the Kammon Straits, between Moji and Shimonoseki, and some through express trains are run. When I was there work was in progress on the extension of the high-speed Shinkansen line from Okayama to an eventual deep-level tunnel under the Kammon Straits, and as far into Kyushu as Hakata. One fears however that when the novelty of very high speed has worn off somewhat, journeys by the 'bullet trains' will lose some of the fascination of train

travel. Between Okayama and Shimonoseki quite half the total mileage will be in tunnel, bored deep into the mountain range of Honshu. The speeds are planned to be even higher than on the original section between Tokyo and Osaka, up to 160 mph; but with long stretches in tunnel the effect on a passenger intent upon sightseeing will be rather breathless and confusing.

A Shinkansen *Hikari* (Lightning) express flashes past Mount Fuji on its southward run from Tokyo to Osaka. These electric trains develop some 16,000 hp. Each axle of every car is motored, enabling the *Hikari* to accelerate from rest to its normal operating speed of 130 mph in about four minutes.

Index

Acknowledgments

*The publishers would like to thank the
following individuals and organizations
for their kind permission to reproduce
the photographs in this book :*

W. J. V. Anderson 17 below, 20–21,
22, 23 above, 23 below, 24 above, 24
below, 24–25, 26 above, 26 below, 27,
29 above, 30, 36–37, 39, 42–43, 44
above, 44 below, 45 above, 45 below,
46, 48 above, 48 below, 49 below, 61,
62–63, 64–65, 65 above, 66–67, 67
above, 68 below, 70 above, 71 below,
92–93, 98–99, 104, 104–105, 106 left,
106–107; Douglass Baglin 121 above;
Yves Broncard 38; Colourviews 7;
Derek Cross 13, 14 below, 15, 16
below; F. Dumbleton 18–19; C. J.
Gammell 8, 10–11, 28 above, 33, 53
above, 58, 59 above, 60–61, 67 below,
68–69, 72, 73 above, 73 centre, 73
below, 74–75, 77 above, 77 below, 94
below, 95; Victor Goldberg 79 below,
83 above, 83 below, 87 above, 87
below, 88–89 below; Victor Hand 81;
Japanese National Tourist Office 126;
J. M. Jarvis 50–51, 52 above, 52 below,
53 below, 79 above, 80, 82 above, 82
below, 84–85, 84 below, 85 below, 90
above, 90 below, 91 below; L. G.
Marshall 76; E. Milne 110–111, 112–
113, 114–115, 115, 118; S. A. Mourton
108–109, 109 above, 109 below, 110,
112, 116–117, 120, 121 below; O. S.
Nock 40 above, 40 below, 89 above
right, 91 above; D. Rodgers 6, 12
above, 12 below, 14 above, 17 above,
28 below, 29 below, 31 above, 32, 59
below, 65 below, 94 above, 97 above,
100–101, 101 above, 102–103; Sakata
Colour Ltd 122–123, 123, 124–125,
124 below; Santa Fe Railroad 78;
Satour 97 below; SNCF (Y. Broncard)
41 above; Union Pacific Railroad
86–87; Western Australia Government Railways 119; C. Whetmath 9,
16 above, 68 above, 70 below, 70–71
above; J. S. Whiteley 10 below, 18,
31 below, 34, 47, 49 above, 54–55, 56
above, 56 below, 56–57; D. Wilkinson
7 above, 28 centre; ZEFA (E. Winters)
35.

Title: Roy Hounsell
Half Title: C. Whetmath
Contents: D. Rodgers
Endpapers and flaps: D. Rodgers